BEYOND
CAPITALISM

BEYOND CAPITALISM

TOWARDS A NEW WORLD ECONOMIC ORDER

KEITH COWLING and ROGER SUGDEN

St. Martin's Press

New York

First published in the United States of America in 1994

Printed in Great Britain

ISBN 0-312-12232-2

Library of Congress Cataloging-in-Publication Data

Cowling, Keith,
    Beyond capitalism: towards a new world economics order / Keith
Cowling and Roger Sugden.
        p.   cm.
    Includes bibliographical references and index.
    ISBN 0-312-12232-2
    1. Economic conditions—1990- 2. Economic policy. 3. Capitalism.
4. International economic relations.   I. Sugden, Roger.   II. Title.
HC59. 15.C69 1994
337—dc20   94-10227
                                                                    CIP

CONTENTS

PREFACE

We have tried to approach this book in a very positive light. We are centrally concerned with identifying a way forward for the organization and management of the world economy. But in order to move in the right direction from where we are today we have to be clear about the deficiencies of the existing system. We therefore spend some time setting out what we see as the essential failures of capitalism as it has matured in the late twentieth century. Partly, this is a reaction to the widespread triumphalism surrounding capitalism following the abrupt demise of state socialism. The total failure of the latter was clear. What appeared less well understood were the limitations of the free market system into which the survivors of state socialism were electing to be decanted. A clearer recognition of the pain which can be inflicted rapidly followed, but without a full understanding of the essence of the system. Neither is the nature of possible alternatives clear nor is it just a matter for the recent entrants to the system. People in Western Europe, the United States, and the other advanced industrial countries have long experienced both the pleasures and the pain of the free market system. In the case of the Third World, most people are perhaps more aware of pain rather than pleasure. There is a widespread view that things could be better and yet no clear idea as to how this can be achieved. We hope this book will play a small role in the process by which a more successful economy and a better society may be created.

We have been greatly aided in the development of the book by many colleagues, students and friends with whom we have exchanged ideas over the years. We would like to mention particularly Patrizio Bianchi, George Chouliarakis, Pat Devine, Paul Geroski, Mark Harrison, Peter Lukacs, Derek Morris, David Parker, Christos Pitelis, Paul Stoneman, Mike Waterson. Keith Cowling would also like to acknowledge the stimulation and help provided by a long line of graduate students at Warwick, some of whom are mentioned above, who were interested in pursuing issues of monopoly capitalism. Teresa Forysiak and Valerie Nash did the word processing. We are grateful to them all.

Keith Cowling
Roger Sugden

Part I
INTRODUCTION

1
THE WORLD ECONOMY IN CRISIS

After 1989 it became fashionable to treat capitalism as triumphantly successful over its twentieth-century adversary, state socialism, with no alternative anywhere in sight. It was a time of rejoicing for the release of people from the oppressive yoke of state bureaucracy and central planning into the freedom and affluence of the Western capitalist system. An unqualified optimism for the market replaced a helpless and sullen acceptance of a failed system for those who had been its prisoners. But while the inadequacies of the so-called socialist system were plain for everyone to see, especially those suffering its direct consequences, it was also the case that for those who cared to look the inadequacies of the system that was so enthusiastically being embraced were equally evident. Obviously, for some the late twentieth-century version of capitalism was proving extremely attractive — particularly so since the 1980s had witnessed enormous redistributions of income, wealth and power in favour of those already possessing these in considerable amounts. And, of course, there are similar examples on the other side — some did very well out of the corrupt and inefficient workings of the system of state socialism. It is also no doubt the case that most people, given the choice, would have elected for the inadequacies of late twentieth-century capitalism in preference to the inadequacies of late twentieth-century state socialism, even if the faults of the former had been fully revealed to them: it may be plausible to argue that 'actually existing socialism', as it was sometimes described, cut too harshly against the grain of core preferences of the individual. Nevertheless it is becoming clear, initially to those most directly affected, that not only is the transition to the capitalist system proving extremely costly, in almost every sense, but that the ultimate objective of this costly process may not be as unambiguously desirable as they once thought. One indication of this was the rejection by the Russian parliament in early 1993 of Yeltsin's free market strategy. But there are also signs within the established capitalist camp of a similar questioning of its ability to deliver the goods. This has always been evident within that part of the world economy, inhabited by a majority of the world's population, where the forces of the capitalist market economy have never revealed any substantially progressive thrust. This would be true, to a greater or lesser extent, of much of the Third World, with some obvious and rather special exceptions. But now, even within the older, advanced industrial economies, there is a rumbling discontent with the political-economic system, and the two elements — politics and economics — cannot easily be dissociated from each other. In the United States this has taken the form of disillusionment with the government. But it is clear that George Bush lost the 1992 (presidential) election because of the state of the economy and his inability, and/or unwillingness, to do anything very much about it, in contrast to his opponent who promised a radical reassessment of economic policy, including possible interventions within the capitalist system which had previously been rejected out of hand. Similarly in Europe there appears to have been a re-emergence of the forces of Eurosclerosis, with the governments of nation states largely ignoring their own electorates and plunging on with the free market, monetarist strategy embedded within economic and political union, although it would appear that the foreign exchange markets have now cast that particular political ambition to the winds. Even Japan is now feeling the effects of the general malaise.

Many will argue that nothing is fundamentally wrong. The problems of the advanced industrial countries will be quickly rectified, either in terms of a normal cyclical recovery, or perhaps within a revised government stance. For the former state socialist economies the situation may be more difficult, but it will be argued that there have been some signs of success and as long as there is no back-sliding everything should come right so long as the advanced industrial countries open up their markets to these emerging capitalist economies. The difficulties of the Third World, although perhaps more deep-seated because of its poorly developed industrial base, are nevertheless put down to the same basic causes: either the internal inability to allow and support the free play of market forces due to corruption, government meddling or even civil war, or the unwillingness of the more advanced countries to allow for the full consequences of such forces in terms of trade. The central belief of many is that capitalism will work if it is allowed to. Among such people there will be different views of the role of government: either it should keep out of the economy altogether, seeking only to set the legal foundations; or it should regulate the market system to avoid undesirable excesses and provide as public goods those services not efficiently provided by the market.

We are not of this persuasion. We see the current crisis as emerging from fundamental difficulties within capitalism and specifically within late twentieth-century capitalism. This book is devoted to the analysis of these fundamental difficulties and to the development of a strategy by which we can move forward to a more satisfactory form of social organization. In the process of our analysis we shall establish that what is wrong with both present-day capitalism, which we shall refer to as monopoly capitalism, and state socialism is their denial of democracy in the full meaning of that term: this denial may appear clear in the case of state socialism, but remains true within capitalism even in the presence of universal suffrage. This denial leads into their inefficiencies and inadequacies. We shall propose measures whereby the present free market system is transformed over a period of time into a democratic market system.

We shall begin in this chapter by describing the present state of the world economy, focusing in turn on the major blocs, North America, Western Europe, Japan and the Pacific Rim, the formerly centrally administered economies of the Soviet Union and Eastern (and Central) Europe, and finally the underdeveloped countries of the Third World. This will in turn require us to probe deeper in Chapter 2, to unearth the major players within the world economy today — the giant transnational corporations. We shall attempt to determine their essence and subsequently their strategy. Chapter 3 examines the consequences for the international economic system of the growth in the power of the transnationals. Whereas many see the international economy as subject to the discipline of international competition, we see it as under the control of the transnationals via their subversion of international trade and investment. Moreover, as will be seen in Chapter 4, this dimension of control implies that the transnationals are able to extend their power base *vis-à-vis* labour and their unions, and *vis-à-vis* communities at various levels (local, regional, national, supranational), via a process of divide and rule. Having established the consequences of the emergence of the dominance of the transnationals in the operation of the free market system, we then examine the macroeconomic effects in Chapter 5. We conclude that these major actors on the world scene inadvertently become the agents of stagnationist forces which ultimately bring about a winding-down of the world economy. At the same time, these same forces render it less likely that political forces will be set in train either to obviate or reverse these tendencies, at least in Keynesian demand-side terms. Given this background the final two chapters (Chapters 6 and 7) seek to develop an economic and political strategy which offers a way forward out of the present morass and beyond the failures of capitalism. It is a strategy aimed fundamentally at transforming the supply-side of the economy by replacing the present free market economy dominated by private concentrations of power with a democratic market economy in which the diffusion of power is a necessary precondition for efficient strategy-making. Chapter 6 concentrates on foundations, while Chapter 7 builds on these foundations by offering an analysis of a series of topical issues: privatization, inward investment, technology, Europe and the regions. This allows the identification of the central characteristics of a New World Economic Order springing from the democratic will rather than being imposed by élitist interests.

Problems in the advanced industrial countries

The contemporary economic problem of the advanced industrial countries of the world, particularly those of Western Europe, is usually identified in terms of persistent, large-scale unemployment, and, since full employment is a legitimate and highly desirable aim, this is indeed an important indicator of economic malaise. However, full employment is clearly not a sufficient description of the absence of economic problems. We seek not only an economic dynamism that enables sustained full employment but also one characterized by a sustained high rate of productivity growth, where such growth fully recognizes, in terms of its measure of output and input, both green issues and the contribution of extra effort in all its dimension. Thus, it is no mindless pursuit of material growth, but one in which the real quality of life is enhanced by both interesting and rewarding employment and the increasing productiveness of such work. We shall also emphasize, in our subsequent analysis of the dominant organization of the free market system, the transnational corporation, and the extent to which the personal development of the individual is constrained by the fundamental characteristics of such organizations. The crucial, strategic decisions within the major corporations are made by a tiny minority of the population. The role of most people is limited and as a result their talents are neither fully used nor fully developed — the capitalist firm is inherently repressive of the creative potential of most individuals. Our focus in this chapter on unemployment and productivity growth as measurable dimensions of an underlying malaise should not blind us to the fact that its source has deep roots within the constraints imposed on human development by the capitalist system.

One level of response to an emerging crisis of large-scale unemployment would be to see it as essentially a demand-side problem, with Keynesian policies as an appropriate reaction. If the appropriate level of aggregate demand for the output of the economy is somehow engineered by government macroeconomic policy then the market will deliver the goods in an efficient manner. Thus if there is a problem with capitalism it can be solved externally; it does not require an intrusion into its inner workings. Whilst we do not want to go into the details of the appropriateness of changes in demand-side policies as a remedy for Eurosclerosis, or the ills of the United States economy, or indeed the current problems in Japan, it is important nevertheless to recognize that whilst appropriate monetary, fiscal and exchange rate policies can make major contributions towards enhancing economic performance, such policies only deal with the symptoms of deeper problems: some medicines may eliminate the symptoms of disease without eliminating the disease itself, thus implying continuing treatment which in itself may not be sustainable, or indeed advisable. Thus, whilst the move away from Keynesian strategies in the mid-1970s in Europe certainly played a significant role in the emergence of Eurosclerosis, reimposing Keynesian solutions now, without a coherent supply-side strategy, would inevitably bring up all the old questions which precipitated the original move away from Keynesianism. This happened in the case of the United Kingdom, with the Lawson 'boom' of 1988 precipitating rising inflation, despite 8 per cent unemployment, and a large balance of payments deficit, despite the much-vaunted, market-based 'supply-side revolution' of the Thatcher decade, incorporating privatization, deregulation, liberalization plus a direct attempt to reduce substantially the power of the trade unions. When put to the test, the British economy appeared not to have the flexibility or enterprise to respond adequately to a quickening in the pace of expansion of demand, and the imports came flooding in, leaving the United Kingdom with a very substantial trade deficit even in the recession years of the early 1990s.

Whilst it can be argued that the British economy is particularly weak because the fundamentals are wrong — with its very narrow manufacturing base, inadequate investment in education, training and modern technology, and despite the more superficial success in manufacturing productivity growth (see, for example, Crafts 1991) — nevertheless it does reveal a general sharpening of the issues surrounding Keynesian reflation. This was also apparent in the short-lived dash for growth by the newly elected socialist administration in France in the early 1980s: as in the more recent case of the United Kingdom, the reflationary policies came to a grinding halt as the trade balance rapidly worsened. The integration of the international economy has moved dramatically on. Simply stimulating demand in one country may have only a limited impact on production in that country, but it will have a major impact on its trade flows, and therefore on its current account balance of payments. For this reason, and for others that will be examined later, national governments tend to be more wary of expansionary demand-side policies and thus unemployment tends to be greater and more persistent whenever the internal workings of the capitalist system generate a tendency towards stagnation.

Turning to the supply side of the economy, there has been much comment on the difference between Europe and the United States in terms of the recent record of unemployment, with the implication that Europe needs to move towards the more flexible labour markets that characterize the US economy. Such a course of action would involve Europe in getting rid of 'high minimum wages, excessive severance pay, heavy fixed costs of employment, restrictions on hiring and firing, support for the closed union shop, meaningless licensing requirements, heavy-handed work-place rules and impediments to geographical mobility' (Blinder 1988). Notice that these arguments are putting the problem within the domain of excessive government — excessive regulation — so that the implicit argument is that if the market were allowed to work then the problem would be solved: there is little wrong with capitalism other than its excessively regulated European form. But what is the evidence that the deregulation of the labour market would bring about the desired result of lower European unemployment? It is certainly the case that the recent record of unemployment in Europe has been much worse than for the United States, with the average rate in Western Europe (members of the Organization for Economic Cooperation and Development) rising from 3 per cent in 1973, the end of the period of relatively full employment stretching back at least to the early 1960s, to 11 per cent in 1986, subsequently falling through 1989, before returning to the

1986 level in the early 1990s; whereas in the case of the United States the rate increased by only two percentage points, from 5 per cent in 1973 to 7 per cent in 1986, with a similar pattern to Europe since then. However, a number of interesting features arise in this particular comparison. First, it appears to be only relatively recently that the maintained greater flexibility of US labour markets has apparently led to a superior performance in terms of lower unemployment, despite the fact that this flexibility is no new phenomenon. Comparing, for example, the United States with the United Kingdom, in the 1960s the United States averaged 4.8 per cent, with the United Kingdom at 1.9 per cent; in the 1970s the United States rate rose to 6.1 per cent, with the United Kingdom rising to 4.3 per cent, and it was only in the 1980s that the ranking was reversed, with the United States at 7.2 per cent and the United Kingdom at 10 per cent (OECD standardized rates). Notice that this reversal of rankings in the 1980s took place despite all the best efforts of Mrs Thatcher to create labour market flexibility by withdrawing government from the regulation of the labour market, whilst at the same time acting decisively to weaken trade union power, with the dramatic defeat of the National Union of Mineworkers providing a powerful image of the new world. This comparison raises crucial questions: if labour market flexibility is important in explaining the level of unemployment, why has it suddenly become so, and, if it has suddenly become so, why does the level of unemployment remain so persistently high in a country, Britain, where active measures have been taken to create flexibility?

A second, dramatic aspect of Western European unemployment is its enormous variation across countries. For example in 1985, unemployment rates ranged from 0.9 per cent in Switzerland to 22 per cent in Spain, and this pattern has tended to show a high degree of persistence (see OECD, *Economic Outlook*, various issues). Nevertheless, it is clear that those with the lowest unemployment rates do not have the flexible labour market characteristics of the United States. Switzerland (unemployment 0.6 per cent in 1990) can be seen as a special case, given that when unemployment threatens it has a policy of returning guest workers to their countries of origin: the problem is exported — a particularly dramatic case of labour market flexibility. Sweden (unemployment 1.5 per cent in 1990), having consistently the second lowest rate of unemployment in Western Europe in recent history, is a more significant case, one described as 'social corporatism' by Glyn and Rowthorn (1988). This system involved the state in active labour market policies allowing industrial jobs to be retained, retraining to take place and wholesale shakeouts to be avoided. As a result Sweden was able to maintain a very low level of unemployment throughout the 1970s and 1980s.

The third point about the comparison between Western Europe and the United States is that the apparent dynamism of the US economy, which created such a growth of employment in the 1970s and 1980s so as to limit the growth of unemployment to a comparatively low level compared with Western Europe, is not manifest in the productivity growth rate of the United States. Over the period 1973–90, productivity growth (measured in terms of Gross Domestic Product (GDP) divided by total employment) averaged only 0.6 per cent per annum for the United States, in contrast to a growth rate of 1.8 per cent per annum in Western Europe (that is OECD Europe; see OECD *Economic Outlook*, Volume 52, 1991). Thus most of the considerable growth rate of US GDP (averaging 2.5 per cent per annum over the same period) is explained by the considerable growth in the employed labour force. As Freeman (1988) has pointed out, per capita GDP (GDP divided by the size of the labour force; that is, employed and unemployed) has grown at similar rates in the United States and in OECD Europe over the 1970s and 1980s, the difference being that, in the United States, there has been greater growth in those doing recorded market work in order to achieve the same overall growth in living standards. Moreover, future living standards will be lower than they otherwise might have been because of the accumulation by the United States of significant debt over this period as the savings of others (particularly Japanese) were used to finance this process of US growth.

The observations made above about Europe and the United States would suggest that: (1) the much-vaunted labour market flexibility of the United States seems not always to have resulted in relatively low unemployment, and attempts to introduce it into Europe seem not to have achieved this particular object;[1] (2) there would appear to be an alternative European model, best exemplified until very recently by Sweden, for achieving full employment; and (3) most of the growth of GDP in the United States has been due to the growth in employment, with productivity growth at a very low level. But if the United States fails to offer a convincing model of the way forward, what of the Swedish way? Glyn and Rowthorn's analysis suggests that since 1973, the date at which unemployment in Western Europe began an upward trend away from a position of fairly full employment achieved in the earlier, post-Second World War period, the growth of Western European unemployment was closely linked to the decline in industrial employment, whereas there appeared to be no signifi-

cant link between overall unemployment and service sector employment. They argue that displaced industrial workers have not been
taken up in service sector employment for such reasons as skill, age,
gender or location. Many countries lost industrial jobs at a rapid rate,
for example Spain, the United Kingdom, Belgium, Ireland, The
Netherlands and France, and such industrial crisis became a crisis of
unemployment. As Glyn and Rowthorn put it, the run-down in
industry created a pool of unemployed which failed to evaporate
because it was not in contact with the central core of the labour
market.

The Swedish model of social corporatism appeared, at first sight, to
offer a way out. The link between industrial crisis and unemployment
crisis was broken by active state intervention in the labour market
involving relatively durable compromises between employers and
employees (see various readings by Goldthorpe 1984). But in the
longer term this is likely to be insufficient. For this sort of corporatist
response to survive — and the Swedish solution has been showing
signs of breaking up with the defeat of the long-established social
democratic ruling party—it would seem necessary to address the
underlying, more fundamental problems that lead to industrial crisis:
the problems which give rise to rapid industrial decline, which in turn
precipitate the problem of structural unemployment.[2] Some indication that these more fundamental problems were not fully addressed
in the Swedish case is provided by its rather poor record on productivity growth, averaging about 0.7 per cent per annum over the
1973–90 period, which was less than half the OECD Europe average
and very similar to the US experience.

If neither the United States nor Sweden offer an adequate model, to
which country can we turn for a more successful model in terms of
managing an essentially capitalist system of production? Or is it the
case that the present capitalist system is such that it cannot be run in a
way that can ensure both full employment and a sustained high rate
of productivity growth? Would such performance now necessitate
such a transformation of the system that it would be no longer recog-
nizable as capitalism and thereby not observable at this time? We
cannot answer these questions at such an early stage, but based on
the record of recent history it is clear that Japan is in a unique position
among the major economies of the advanced capitalist world in providing both full employment and a relatively rapid rate of productivity growth.[3] Employment growth over the 1970s and 1980s was
almost sufficient to maintain full employment (the unemployment
rate for 1990 was 2.1 per cent, in contrast to OECD Europe with 8 per

cent and the United States with 5.4 per cent; see OECD *Economic Outlook*, Volume 53, 1992), whilst at the same time a considerable rate of productivity growth (3 per cent per annum for the period 1973–90) was maintained, well in advance of Japan's major industrial rivals, as we have already seen. It is also necessary in establishing the significance of this performance to remember that it was achieved despite this period of history being a particularly traumatic one for Japan, faced as it was with an oil and commodity price explosion to which it was particularly exposed and over which it had little control (unlike its major rivals whose corporations play a dominant role in these international markets), and more recently with a dramatic appreciation of the yen, which might have been expected to weaken its previously very strong position in international trade.

Clearly the Japanese economy differs in many ways from the Western European and US economies, but one of the differences is of particular interest in the present context: Japan has a coherent, strategic industrial policy unlike any other major advanced capitalist economy, although some countries come closer to it than others.[4] Japan can be seen as the most important case of the government taking on a central developmental role in the economy without directly owning most of the productive assets, that is, outside of what was referred to as state socialism. The success of the Japanese economy since 1945 is obvious: Japan was able to establish a remarkable dynamism over an extended period, which we believe has not been extinguished despite the present financial crisis. But the question arises to what extent the Japanese success story relates to the government's industrial strategy, that is, the extent to which capitalist market forces were shaped by the intervention of government agency. A debate has raged on this question at least since the early 1970s without reaching any clear-cut solution. This is not surprising since orthodox economics offers only limited accommodation to ideas of industrial strategy-making. Nevertheless a number of observers from outside mainstream economics — from political science (for instance, Johnson 1982; Reich 1983, 1991), from sociology (Dore 1986), as well as, of course, from more heterodox positions within the economics profession (for example, Best 1990; Kobayashi 1993; Ozaki 1984) — have looked at the government's role in the Japanese economy and come to the view that it has been important to explain its comparative success.

The Japanese case is a very significant one, constituting as it does a major, successful challenge to the world economic dominance of the United States and Western Europe. But its significance goes deeper.

There was a recognition within Japan that the market cannot be left to achieve this breakthrough by itself. The creation of a successful economy in the second half of the twentieth century required the intrusion by government into its inner workings. Catch-up is not automatic, but neither is full employment and sustained productivity growth when you are a leading economy. The examples we have looked at would suggest that free market economies may tend to stagnate — they certainly do not tend to utilize efficiently the resources available. Our observations on this point would suggest the possibility of a dual-track, supply-side policy for the advanced industrial countries, with an active labour market policy along the lines of the Swedish model aimed at avoiding short-term industrial unemployment, leading into a coherent industrial strategy, learning from Japanese experience, guiding the longer-term evolution of the industrial economy, directed at dynamic growth. But we shall need to take our analysis forward on a number of fronts before we can present more specific proposals.

Continuing problems in the Third World

It is not necessary to dwell at length on establishing the case for the failure of capitalism in the context of the Third World. Almost by definition this huge area of the world with its huge population has lost out in the process of economic development. Income levels generally are desperately low, poverty abounds, people are either underemployed or working long hours for a pittance. This is the most demonstrable waste within the capitalist system. As a dramatic illustration of the lack of development, the average per capita income (Gross National Product) of the developing economies in 1990[5] was just US$800 in contrast to the figure of US$18,330 within the developed economies (High Income Economies). But, of course, the average for the developing economies conceals substantial diversity. An area of the world that has done particularly badly in recent years, Sub-Saharan Africa, recorded an average per capita income for 1989 of US$340, and South Asia, which has done comparatively well recently, recorded a level of only US$320. Comparisons of living standards across countries are exceedingly difficult to make (see Summers and Heston 1991), but it is clear that the world capitalist system has failed to deliver anything close to a reasonable standard of life for a very considerable fraction of the world's population.

Now, of course, people will point to limitations of natural resources and to a range of political, social and cultural factors which may have impeded the processes of development, and undoubtedly a detailed country-by-country analysis could reveal lots of these. But it remains a fact that more than a century has passed since Western Europe and the United States entered a period of sustained economic develop-ment (see, for example, Crafts 1985), and much of the world appears not to have been fully absorbed into this process, or at least into the progressive elements of such development: clearly most of the world has been significantly affected by the economic forces emanating from Europe and the United States, but not in a way which has led to a cumulative process of catch-up.[6]

Given this picture of a world economy under capitalism which, while achieving much in terms of the evolution of living standards in certain favoured areas, has at the same time left most of the world underdeveloped or undeveloped, it would at first sight seem para-doxical that in recent years the dominant paradigm within develop-ment economics has become one which advocates unrelenting capitalist forces — the unadulterated free market — for the resolution of the problems of the Third World. As Fishlow (1991) remarks, 'The impact of the new emphasis upon markets is nowhere so dramatic as in development economics'. From being a problem of capitalism the tables have been neatly turned: the villain of the piece is not capi-talism, but the lack of it, not market forces, but their excessive regula-tion. As elsewhere, in the advanced industrial countries, whether capitalist or formerly centrally administered, as in the case of Central and Eastern Europe and the former Soviet Union, privatization, liber-alization and deregulation are the order of the day. And as with Central and Eastern Europe and the former Soviet Union, this solu-tion is promoted by the two dominant supranational organizations of the world economy, the International Monetary Fund and the World Bank, significantly the organizations of the West, particularly the United States currently so hamstrung by those same forces. Faced by balance of payments difficulties and consequent serious foreign exchange constraints, these countries of the Third World and the former Soviet Empire have turned for help to the IMF and the World Bank which have in turn responded by imposing two sets of condi-tions: first, an increase in the role of free markets and private enter-prise, and a general rolling-back of the state, and, second, a closer integration with the world economy, implying the liberalization of imports and inward investment (see, for example, Singh 1992). But is this an appropriate way forward? Is this the way out of grinding poverty for these countries? Is it enough to roll back the state in its present form and substitute the market? At this point we simply examine the empirical evidence provided by the varied history of Third World economies to see whether there appears to be a case for such prescriptions. We shall examine this both over time and across countries.

We have already established the very low levels of income per capita in the Third World today; nevertheless, the three decades after the Second World War constituted a 'Golden Age of development for the poor countries of the world' (Singh 1993). It was a time when political and economic conditions were ripe for the start of an industrial revolution in many of these countries. Rapid economic growth in the advanced industrial economies, coupled with the break-up of empire, provided suitable conditions for this long-delayed transformation to take place. But the beginnings of a process of transformation did not take place spontaneously. 'The economic development doctrine of that day explained why laissez faire had not worked, and could not work, and how a more active state role could compensate' (Fishlow 1991). The history of this period repeated the history of the earlier patterns of industrialization in Western Europe, the United States and Japan: in each case, with the unique exception of the powerful prime mover, Britain, the state had been actively and purposively involved in the transformation. Indeed, the Japanese have stated that they learnt their approach to industrial policy-making from the experiences of the United States in the nineteenth century (Johnson 1984).

Over the past decade the development process has appeared to stall. Whilst during the period 1965–73 the Third World economies achieved an average productivity growth of 4.3 per cent p.a. (GNP per capita), they moderated to 2.7 per cent p.a. during 1973–80, and fell sharply to 1.2 per cent in the 1980s. It is in the light of this recent poor performance that the new development paradigm has been enunciated. And yet we have the Golden Age to explain: if a strong state involvement in development proved generally beneficial over the first thirty years, why should it be called into question over the last ten? Of course, there may still be a 'government failure' case to answer, perhaps based on an institutional ossification, and our investigation of cross-country diversity may throw light on this, but when considering the diversity of performance over time it might seem more obvious to examine changes in external forces that may strongly impinge on performance in the Third World. If so, we do not have far to look. It has been widely argued that the debt crisis within the Third

World, which affected Latin America particularly, was the main reason for the breakdown in development in the 1980s and that this debt crisis resulted from external economic forces over which these countries lacked control (see Singh 1993 for a survey of the literature). The evolution of highly restrictionist monetarist policies within the advanced industrial economies at the end of the 1970s led directly to higher interest rates and indirectly to a worsening in terms of trade for Third World countries. In so far as the policies led to a reduction in growth in the advanced industrial economies, there was also a reduction in the demand for Third World exports. The commodity terms of trade (commodity price index ÷ manufacturers price index) showed a deterioration of 35 per cent between 1978–80 and 1986–88, a quite remarkable fall: the decline in the corresponding index during the Great Depression was both less severe and less prolonged (Maizels 1992). Is it surprising that countries heavily reliant on commodity exports might have difficulties maintaining the rate of development when faced with such enormous shocks? It is hardly a reason for exposing these countries to even more market shocks, but it perhaps provides a strong argument for establishing greater governmental, or joint governmental, control over such markets. It is surely significant to note that these commodity markets are typically controlled by a few buyers with their origins within the advanced industrial countries. Maizels (1992) reports that between three and six transnational corporations control 90 per cent of coffee exports; 88 per cent of tea exports; 85 per cent of cocoa exports; and 85–90 per cent of jute exports (of course, different groups in each case) — just the sort of oligopsonistic control that is quite able to exploit periods of excess supply to its own advantage.

Thus we are suggesting that the observed variation in economic performance over time in the Third World has more to do with events outside the control of the Third World governments than with any deterioration in the performance of such governments. It may therefore be inappropriate to respond to the observed recent deterioration in performance by requiring a rolling-back of the state as a condition for dispensing capital funding. But what about the diversity in performance across countries — does that point towards free market solutions? Certainly it is the case, as with the advanced industrial economies, that we observe an enormous variation in performance across countries; indeed, the diversity in performance is substantially magnified in the case of the Third World.

Some countries have been able to establish a real economic dynamism. Particular attention has focused on the Four Dragons —

South Korea, Taiwan, Singapore and Hong Kong — and for good reason. Each has achieved a remarkable productivity growth rate over an extended period. Both South Korea and Singapore averaged a growth rate of Gross National Product per capita of 7 per cent over the period 1965–89 and Hong Kong and Taiwan (for 1952–89) were close behind at 6.3 per cent (World Bank 1991; Asian Development Outlook 1991; Lim 1988). For a considerable period the experiences of these countries were taken as strong evidence in favour of the innate dynamism of free market economies (Chen 1979; Wolf 1988). Then people started to examine these economies a little more closely. It became apparent that they could not adequately be described as free market economies — in each case government was taking an active, variable, but quite central role (Lim 1983; White 1988; Amsden 1989; Wade 1990b; Westphal 1990). In South Korea, Taiwan and Singapore the active role of government is very clear and yet they have followed quite different development modes. While South Korea has relied to a considerable extent on the development of giant private firms, strongly backed by the state, Taiwan has relied much more on public enterprise at the leading edge. In contrast to both, Singapore has been much more directly reliant on foreign-based, transnational corporations for capital investment, with 83 per cent of manufacturing production controlled by them, compared with a figure of 11 per cent for South Korea (Dicken 1986). This particular characteristic of Singaporean development seems to have led to specific difficulties. It could be argued that of these three countries Singapore was in the best position to exploit development opportunities in the post-Second World War period, since it was already well entrenched in the capitalist world economy as an entrepôt port with a highly developed network of commercial activities. But after a rapid early start in industrialization, things began to falter in the early 1980s. The transnationals started to move out to lower-cost South Pacific locations, so that at a time when South Korea and Taiwan continued their rapid progress, Singapore experienced negative growth (e.g. –2.8 per cent in 1985). However, the government intervened with some vigour, led the economy into high technology activities, and moved it back to its high growth trajectory.

So much for three of the dragons, where there have been different modes of development, but where government has in each case taken a strong leadership role. But what of Hong Kong? Its success is taken by some as evidence that industrial policy in the other three economies may not be as important in their success as is being claimed by those favouring government intervention in the processes of development. Has not Hong Kong been as close to a free market economy as it is possible to get? And has it not been equally successful? Wade (1990a) offers an answer in three parts. First, Hong Kong is special in terms of size and development prior to industrialization and also because of its position as a gateway to China. Second, it is a variant of a guided market economy and it is misleading to consider it to be close to a free market economy: the close linkages between the major banks, trading companies and colonial government allow for a development strategy without formal institutions. And third, more recently, Hong Kong may not have done as well as the others due to a slower rate of restructuring of its export base. Whilst it is difficult to isolate the cause, given the uncertainty surrounding Hong Kong's future, the problem was recognized in the 1987 proposals by the Hong Kong government on 'radical departure'. This new initiative includes 'developmental support', with help with training and technology in certain areas of electronics. There seems to have been a conversion to a strategy of creating winners.

We have to conclude that the most outstanding examples of dynamism emerging from the post-Second World War Third World economy were not free market economies: as with the case of Japan, the most dramatic example of economic dynamism within the advanced industrial countries, rapid development was achieved within a 'guided' market economy, in the context of a 'strategic' integration with the world economy. The rules of the IMF/World Bank were violated and economic success was achieved. Thus the argument about the role of the state has to be made 'not in terms of the extent, but rather with respect to the nature and quality of the government interventions' (Singh 1993). Indeed, the World Bank (1991) now recognizes the important role of the state in economic development, but reduces that role to creating a suitable environment for private enterprise. This is a quite inadequate description of the leading, proactive role which government assumed in the case of Japan and the Four Dragons. It is also not the case in China, which has achieved a similar dynamism; particularly impressive has been the rapid growth of small-scale industry in rural areas as a form of municipal socialism (Nolan 1991). What may be true is that problems can arise when the state tends to reduce its role to that advocated by the World Bank, as is suggested in the case of Singapore and Hong Kong.

However, it is undoubtedly true that the presence of government within the economy is no guarantee of good performance. There are many disastrous examples in the Third World, as with Central and Eastern Europe and the former Soviet Union, involving overly centralized, bureaucratic and indeed corrupt administrations. Whilst in many cases life for interventionist government in the Third World was made difficult by a variety of interventions by Western capitalist economies and their political institutions, it remains true that there were and are many administrations around the world, whether proclaiming socialism or not, that had an essentially negative impact on development, sometimes despite the best of motives. The lesson to be drawn appears to be that, just as we do not deny the market because of instances of market failure, neither should we deny government because of instances of government failure. 'Free' market economies do not appear capable of matching the performance of 'guided' market economies, where such guidance derives from a serious attempt to cultivate competence in this activity. What is necessary is a subtle blend of '... private and public entrepreneurialism ...' (Lim 1988). The development mode of the star performers suggests a central role for government within a market economy, but at this point we are drawing lessons from observation rather than from analysis. Whilst star performers may offer useful pointers to a new and better economic order, there should be no presumption that they have achieved anything which is in a general sense an optimum. Further understanding on this front awaits a fundamental analysis of the organization of production, an issue to which we turn in later chapters. But before moving on to such analysis it is perhaps instructive briefly to assess the nature of the current transition of the former centrally administered economies of Central and Eastern Europe and the Soviet Union into capitalist market economies.

Transitional problems in Central and Eastern Europe and the former Soviet Union

Since 1989 we have observed a depressing vista of economic disintegration and collapse as the formerly centrally administered economies of Central and Eastern Europe and the former Soviet Union have progressively opened themselves up to the processes and structures of free market capitalism. By the end of 1992 output had fallen by between 16 per cent and 42 per cent respectively, and, in all cases except Poland,[7] showed every sign of further reductions. This is an unprecedented state of affairs and calls into question the nature of the transition and its ultimate objective. It could be argued that in all these cases variations on a big bang approach to a transition to capi-

talist market economies were undertaken, with the 'rapid liberalization of the goods and foreign exchange markets' as the core element
(Borensztein 1993). It appears that this *laissez-faire* approach to a
laissez-faire economy has resulted in a dramatic dislocation of production and an enormous loss of output. Although the advocates of this
approach did not warn of these losses in the transition, it could be
argued that a headlong rush into unknown territory, as was being
proposed, was bound to result in such dislocation. These countries
were simply bereft of the institutional structures of capitalism and
thus to open up their economies to world capitalist forces would
inevitably leave them very exposed. Whether big bang, gradualism, or
particular mixed strategies are appropriate we shall leave until later,
but what we might conclude at this point is that relatively unrestricted
market forces have brought chaos to an important segment of the
world economy, a chaos that might have been avoided had a more
strategic integration into the world capitalist economy on Japanese
lines been followed (see Singh 1993). The evidence of Japan would
also suggest that the final destination of the transition would be a
guided market economy rather than a so-called free one. The recent
experience of China and Vietnam is also supportive of this view.
Whilst output in the transitional economies in Central and Eastern
Europe and the former Soviet Union has been spiralling down, the
state socialist economies of East Asia (for example, China and
Vietnam) have been flourishing under a more guided transition, with
output growth rates averaging about 10 per cent p.a. The difference in
experience is dramatic, but it will be argued that '... political circumstances and the structure of the economy' dictated the differences in
strategy (Borensztein 1993). One must accept that there exist substantial political and economic differences between the two groups of
countries. However, it is necessary to add that the pressure imposed
by the IMF and the World Bank on the governments of Central and
Eastern Europe and the former Soviet Union for a rapid integration
into the world economy and a rapid privatization of state assets was a
telling element in those differences (see, for example, the implicit conditionality attached to the Russian Loan as reported by the IMF
Managing Director, Michel Camdessus, *IMF Survey*, 12 July 1993). The
other point that needs to be made about the comparison is that it is
not correctly described as big bang versus gradualism. There is every
indication that the East Asian transitional economies are being rapidly
and radically restructured (see, for example, Peter Nolan 1991), so in
this sense it is a big bang transition, but in contrast to the transitional
economies elsewhere the process is within the context of an overall

industrial strategy. The transition to a market economy is being planned.

The theme of the book

The observations we have made of the world economy suggest the existence of fundamental problems within capitalism as it has evolved in the second half of the twentieth century. The triumphalism following the fall of state socialism has been short-lived. Within the advanced industrial economies unemployment seems endemic and long-term productivity growth is generally poor; the Third World is in continuing crisis, as are the transitional economies of Central and Eastern Europe and the former Soviet Union. However, we were also able to observe islands of hope within the generally depressing scene, in economies like Japan, the Four Dragons of the Pacific Rim, and China. Whilst these economies are in many ways very different from each other, nevertheless they have a crucial element in common: none of them can be accurately described as free market economies. It appears that the depressing economic scene is relieved only where we observe a deep intrusion by the state, in some way representing the broader polity, within the inner workings of the capitalist economy or, in China's case, in guiding the economy towards the market. These observations receive support from economically dynamic regions within underperforming nations. The most famous case is the area in and around Emilia Romagna, the so-called Third Italy, where regional and local government is intimately involved in the economic development process (see, for example, Best 1990). Nevertheless, this is not meant to imply that the intrusion of government into the actual functioning of the capitalist economy will be necessarily beneficial — there are clearly numerous instances of government failure — rather, it is to suggest that the star performers are better described as guided market economies than free market economies. However, there can be no presumption that what we observe represent socially optimal arrangements, nor would it be legitimate to argue that other economies should seek to imitate the development mode of star performers: indeed, there is considerable variation in such modes. To take things further we need to probe the roots of the problems of free market economies — only then can we begin to design alternative structures that offer the prospect of better economic performance.

It is important to emphasize that the crisis we observe besetting the capitalist economy is world-wide; it is not just a British crisis, or a Russian or United States crisis, or a Third World crisis, but a crisis of the capitalist system as a whole. Thus we must turn to the characteristics of the world economic system as a whole to unravel an explanation; we cannot simply look at national characteristics to explain something that is a world-wide phenomenon. Inevitably this means we have to turn to the dominant agents that span that system. We suggest that the present reality of the free market economy is that it is dominated by giant economic organizations with a transnational base: the transnational corporations. We have already seen an example of this dominance in the case of world commodity markets (Maizels 1992). As a consequence of this dominance, we shall argue that markets are controlled and manipulated by a powerful subset of the population — the few who control the transnationals. This élite influences situations and events for its own benefit and hence observed outcomes will be optimal for some but not for society as a whole. As a consequence a free market economy is a socially inefficient economy. This is not a problem of markets *per se*, rather a problem with the way markets are used by the powerful to further their own interests.

Given this reality of the free market economy, it is natural for us, in the next chapter, to consider the essence of the transnational corporation, indeed the essence of the capitalist firm. We define a transnational corporation as a means of coordinating production from one centre of strategic decision-making when this coordination takes the firm across national boundaries. Thus the boundaries of the firm are no longer defined in terms of ownership, but in terms of control over production, either directly or through the market, for example, via subcontracting. We then proceed to consider why transnationals are created in the first place and to examine the effect of transnationalism on product market domination. We argue that the development of a transnational system of production by the giant corporation gives it an added dimension of power within any specific market.

Chapter 3 focuses directly on the international economic system *per se*, as against its major players, the transnational corporations. It suggests that production activities are more or less spread throughout the world according to the relative attraction of particular locations for achieving the objectives of firms' strategic decision-makers, but that strategic decision-making itself is very highly concentrated. Having considered the variation in structure and organization across different transnationals, we highlight further consequences of the presence of transnationals: subversion of international trade, centripetalism and short-termism.

Chapter 4 takes up the issue of divide and rule, thereby analysing two further deficiencies of the capitalist economic system. Its prime concern is the divide and rule of labour; it explores the fundamental asymmetry between capital and labour, given that capital is organized internationally and labour is not. The second deficiency analysed in Chapter 4 is the divide and rule of governments, the idea that transnationals increase profits by playing off governments in different nations and regions.

The impact of the tendency for the share of wages to fall (predicted in Chapter 2) is analysed in Chapter 5. We argue that a secular stagnation will tend to result as a consequence of a decline in the growth of aggregate demand. Complementary to such demand-side explanation of stagnation, we also develop supply-side arguments for the emergence of such tendencies in the advanced industrial countries as transnational capital migrates to other, lower-cost locations. We argue for the social inefficiency of such deindustrialization processes. We also conclude that stagnation becomes a more pressing issue where transnational control is on the increase because it will become more unmanageable within the context of national policy-making.

Having examined the roots of the deficiencies of the world free market economy, we turn, in the final two chapters, to the more positive side of the book. An obvious response to our analysis of deficiencies in capitalism is to address the most fundamental cause for concern: the socially incomplete decision structure of the capitalist firm. We suggest that a firm can only serve the interests of a community more widely if more of the members of that community are involved in its strategic decisions, that is, if there is greater democracy. A prime task for economists is then to design policies by which this can be achieved. We advocate a planned process, but not central planning; the idea of central planning is in many ways diametrically opposed to the diffused and deconcentrated economy we seek, given our overall aim of greater democracy. It is argued that markets, being sometimes effective mechanisms for allocating scarce resources, can become a tool for communities as against being a tool for the élite in a free market system. It is also argued that government will need to play a constant role in moving the economy towards a more diffuse, less concentrated structure of decision-making.

Finally we address the international dimensions of this new economic order, one in which political democracy is enhanced by a widening and deepening of economic democracy. Whilst our central concern is to create meaningful regional economies, containing within themselves the linkages, diversity and decision-making power to secure a substantial degree of self-determination, nevertheless it is important to preserve and enhance linkages with other communities, establishing the significance of a wider democracy and a wider community. We envisage an outward-looking rather than introverted approach, on grounds of equity, with richer communities supporting poorer, but also on grounds of efficiency, given that introverted societies can lose impetus and momentum without the stimuli of outside influences. Thus we end with a call for a new international economic order based on a network of relatively autonomous communities where cooperation among successful economies displaces the competition based on fear of the present order. We would commend a true internationalism growing out of a firm base of community autonomy at local, regional and national level, rather than the present internationalism designed in the interest of the few.

Notes

1 It is interesting to speculate whether what was achieved in the United Kingdom was rather a more rapid advance in productivity growth (see, for example, Crafts 1991), but one in which the rate of displacement of people from employment was also increased, thus contributing to rising unemployment and a limited impact of productivity growth on the growth of output.
2 None of this is meant to deny that structural change is often necessary, but rather to emphasize that such change should be paced to allow for the efficient adaptation of the labour force to the changing composition of employment opportunities. A sufficient dynamism in the industrial sector will tend to maintain industrial jobs as well as generating significant productivity growth.
3 One potentially important qualification may be in order. It has been suggested at various times that the Japanese government has sought to control migration from agriculture in order to avoid a higher level of recorded unemployment. We are not in a position to judge the importance of such policy.
4 The United States and the United Kingdom would come at one end of the scale, with little in the nature of an overall industrial strategy despite having a whole variety of specific industrial policies, and France, Germany and the European Union at the other end, at least with elements of a coherent strategy. Outside the major advanced industrial economies we have further examples of coherent strategy making which will be examined later.

5 World Bank (1991), 'Low and Middle Income Economies', Table A.2, p. 182, see Definitions and Notes.
6 Over the last quarter of the century there is evidence that the Third World is breaking up into two groups, one in which the forces of sustained development have taken hold, the other where undevelopment continues (see, for example, Dowrick and Gemmell 1991). We shall have more to say on this.
7 However, note that, according to Gomulka (1991), a return to the pre-reform level of GDP in Poland is unlikely before 1995: that is six years of enormous losses in output (with 1990: –12 per cent; 1991: –10 per cent).

Part II
THE FAILURES OF CAPITALISM

2
THE MAJOR PLAYERS: THE GIANT TRANSNATIONALS

We have argued in the previous chapter that there is a lack of dynamism in the world economic system. This has been evidenced by focusing on various countries in the major blocs, North America, Western Europe, Japan and the Pacific Rim, the formerly centrally administered economies of the Soviet Union and Eastern (and Central) Europe, and the underdeveloped countries of the Third World. The crisis in the world economy is not a problem peculiar to a particular nation; rather it is an international issue.

In this and the subsequent chapters we will explore deficiencies in the world economy in considerable detail. Hence we will examine and clarify one of this book's central arguments, namely that economies across the world have failed the communities they purport to serve and that they will inevitably continue to do so unless fundamental changes are introduced. More specifically, we will suggest that the so-called free market process that is the essence of capitalism is a process dominated by an élite. The result is necessarily the optimization of private interests and social inefficiency.

Our particular concern throughout this part of the book will be to analyse the nature and impact of the giant transnational corporations. The reason for this focus is that these firms are the major players in the world economy. It is the realization that we are dealing with a crisis in the world economy and not simply a particular nation that intuitively points to the significance of focusing on these major players. Our subsequent analysis will support this intuition with detailed theoretical and empirical argument.

According to the United Nations, transnational corporations are 'central actors' in the world economy (United Nations 1993). Moreover, although it has been estimated that at the beginning of the 1990s there were over 37,000 transnationals world-wide (ibid.), it is the largest of these firms that account for much of transnationals' activity; for example, data published in the mid-1980s suggested that fifty of the largest transnationals accounted for approximately 35 per cent of total foreign production (i.e. production outside a firm's 'home' boundaries), and that 500 of the largest accounted for 75 per cent of the total (Dunning 1993). Further evidence on the scale of transnationals' presence will be considered later in this chapter. However, we will then go on to, in a sense, less superficial matters, to explore the nature and essence of the typical giant transnational. We will consider what is meant by the term transnational corporation and begin to examine why a firm chooses to produce in various countries. Strategic decision-making will be identified as especially important and we will point to the élite making those decisions as especially influential. Out of this analysis we will conclude the chapter by beginning to discuss the consequences of transnationals' presence. Our focus will be on product market monopolization, particularly the so-called degree of monopoly. This will entail a general discussion of the determinants of the degree of monopoly and then a more specific discussion of transnationals' influence. It will be suggested that the presence of giant transnational corporations implies systemic problems associated with product market monopolization.

The scale of transnationals' presence

Down the years there has been a great deal of interesting information reported about the scale of transnationals' activities, and indeed it is relatively easy to show that transnationals are significant players in the world's economies without attempting to be anywhere near exhaustive in presenting the available data.

The overwhelming concern in published information is the overseas activities of 'domestic' transnationals or the domestic activities of 'overseas' transnationals. In this spirit, Table 2.1 reports evidence on transnationals' foreign direct investment (crudely, equity investment outside a firm's home country in production activity over which it exerts significant influence; see Dunning 1993 for a discussion of the term). The table shows inward and outward investment stocks in 1990. The inward stock of all developed countries was over $1230 billion and the outward stock over $1602 billion. The magnitudes for developing countries in total were far smaller but the inward stock, at approximately $266 billion, swamped the outward stock, approximately $11 billion. One thing the table does not report is the concentration across firms but on this point it is interesting to record the United Nations (1993) estimate that the largest 100 transnationals hold approximately one-third of the world-wide stock of foreign direct investment.

To provide some feel for the relative significance of such investments, Table 2.2 focuses on inward foreign direct investment for various years over the period 1980–90. The table covers the same set of countries as does Table 2.1. The share of foreign affiliates in both exports and total sales is consistently very high (in excess of 25 per cent) across all of the countries reported. For instance, foreign affiliates accounted for 26 per cent of French and 38 per cent of UK exports, with similar and even higher figures in developing countries, notably Singapore (86 per cent) and Malaysia (46 per cent). There are also some high shares for foreign affiliates in total assets, employment, value-added and profit, for example, a 25 per cent assets share in Canada, a 43 per cent employment share in Ireland, a 28 per cent value-added share in Indonesia, and a 43 per cent profit share in Brazil. Moreover, examining Tables 2.1 and 2.2 side by side provides quite strong evidence of transnationals' presence. In Table 2.1, some countries stand out as having especially large stocks of inward and outward investment in absolute terms — notably Australia, Canada, France, Germany, Italy, Japan, the United Kingdom and the United States, each with a combined inward and outward stock of foreign direct investment in excess of $100 billion. Yet it is clear from Table 2.2 that the influence of transnationals spreads far beyond these eight nations. For instance, the stock of inward investment in Argentina was approximately $7 billion in 1989 — compared to $206 billion and $404 billion in the United Kingdom and United States at similar times — yet at various points from the mid-1980s to the early 1990s inward foreign direct investment had a share in Argentinian exports, employment, value-added and sales of 37 per cent, 27 per cent, 27 per cent and 52 per cent respectively.

Furthermore, interesting though such data are, it does not tell us everything about the scale of transnationals' presence. For one thing, the data underlying Tables 2.1 and 2.2 rely on equity investments above a certain (unspecified) threshold as the basis for identifying transnationals' activities; the idea is that foreign direct investment refers to a firm exerting significant influence over production activity

Table 2.1 Stocks of inward and outward foreign direct investment by transnational corporations, various countries, 1990 ($m.)

Country	Inward stock	Outward stock
All developed countries	1,230,215	1,602,199
All developing countries	265,899	10,781
Australia	74,451[a]	27,357[a]
Austria	6,816[b]	1,360[b]
Belgium/Luxembourg	28,588[c]	22,651[c]
Canada	108,023	74,703
Denmark	9,192	10,441
Finland	4,112[c]	8,188[c]
France	51,121[c]	74,833[c]
Germany	93,456	155,133
Ireland	5,405[c]	—
Italy	57,985	56,105
Japan	18,432	310,808
New Zealand	3,242[c]	2,322[c]
Norway	2,450[b]	2,757[b]
Portugal	2,019[b]	199[b]
Sweden	7,309[b]	24,850[b]
Turkey	1,320	—
UK	205,618[b]	244,753
USA	403,735	423,183
Fiji	310[c]	—
Hong Kong	11,685[c]	—
Indonesia	38,883	—
Malaysia	10,117[b]	1,878[b]
Pakistan	1,254[b]	228[b]
Philippines	1,568[c]	154[b]
Republic of Korea	3,956[b]	1,119[b]
Singapore	26,780[c]	—
Sri Lanka	618[b]	—
Thailand	5,536[c]	258[c]
Argentina	6,942[c]	—
Brazil	37,143	2,397
Colombia	3,500	402
Paraguay	253[b]	—
Peru	1,254	63
Uruguay	459[c]	—
Ghana	375	—
Mauritius	66[b]	—
Zimbabwe	2,122[c]	—

[a] 1991.
[b] 1988.
[c] 1989.
Source: United Nations (1993).

Table 2.2 The relative importance of inward foreign direct investment, various countries, 1980–90 (%)

Country	Exports	Assets	Employment	Value-added	Sales	Profits
			Share of foreign affiliates in total			
Australia	—	—	—	—	—	22.6 (1983)
Austria	—	—	13.5 (1985)	—	—	—
Belgium/Luxembourg	—	—	18.0 (1985)	—	39.8 (1985)	—
Canada	—	25.0 (1990)	—	—	25.8 (1990)	26.6 (1990)
Denmark[a]	—	11.6 (1986)	12.4 (1986)	14.2 (1986)	13.3 (1986)	13.2 (1986)
Finland	—	—	4.4 (1988)	—	—	—
France[a]	25.9 (1982)	—	20.2 (1982)	—	25.3 (1982)	—
Germany (West)	—	—	8.3 (1982)	—	—	—
Ireland[a]	—	—	42.8 (1987)	—	65.0 (1987)	—
Italy	—	—	11.8 (1985)	—	—	—
Japan	—	0.8 (1986)	0.4 (1986)	1.0 (1986)	—	—
New Zealand	—	—	—	—	—	28.9 (1980)
Norway	—	—	4.0 (1981)	—	—	—
Portugal	—	—	8.2 (1984)	—	—	—
Sweden	—	—	—	—	—	11.1 (1988)
Turkey	—	—	2.0 (1988)	—	—	—
UK	38.0 (1988)	—	—	—	—	10.0 (1988)
USA	—	13.2[a] (1987)	3.7 (1987)	4.3 (1987)	11.4[a] (1987)	5.9[a] (1987)
Fiji	35.6 (1985)	—	25.0 (1985)	44.0 (1985)	40.6 (1985)	56.9 (1985)
Hong Kong	—	17.7 (1986)	5.4[a] (1987)	—	7.1[a] (1987)	—
Indonesia[a]	—	—	10.9 (1980)	27.6 (1980)	—	—

Table 2.2 Continued

Country	Exports	Assets	Share of foreign affiliates in total Employment	Value-added	Sales	Profits
Malaysia	45.7 (1988)	19.0 (1988)	32.2 (1988)	—	31.4 (1988)	45.7 (1988)
Pakistan	6.0 (1988)	—	—	—	—	—
Philippines	34.7 (1987)	18.9 (1987)	2.7 (1987)	—	26.0 (1987)	30.8 (1987)
Republic of Korea	29.0 (1986)	—	2.7 (1986)	—	—	—
Singapore	86.1[a] (1988)	—	59.5[a] (1988)	71.7 (1989)	53.0[a] (1988)	—
Sri Lanka	26.2 (1987)	—	—	—	—	—
Thailand	—	16.3 (1986)	—	—	39.3 (1986)	—
Argentina	37.3 (1990)	—	26.8[a] (1984)	26.8[a] (1984)	51.6 (1988)	—
Brazil	26.7[a] (1987)	—	16.2 (1987)	—	17.7 (1987)	43.3 (1987)
Colombia[a]	22.8 (1987)	—	12.0 (1987)	24.8 (1987)	—	—
Paraguay	20.1 (1988)	—	—	—	—	—
Peru	25.3[b] (1988)	—	6.5 (1989)	57.2[c] (1988)	51.1[c] (1988)	13.5 (1988)
Uruguay[a]	—	—	—	—	13.6 (1987)	—
Ghana[a]	—	—	48.4 (1986)	48.4 (1986)	45.7 (1986)	—
Mauritius	—	—	65.4 (1984)	—	—	—
Zimbabwe[a]	—	25.3 (1988)	—	—	—	—

[a]Secondary sector.
[b]Primary sector.
[c]Primary and secondary sectors.

Source: United Nations (1992).

outside its home country, and that such influence requires an equity holding above a certain level. This is very restrictive, as will be implied when we subsequently explore the concept of a transnational corporation, but as is also recognized in the existing literature. For example, United Nations (1993) observes that in practice:

firms carry out their transnational activities and exert control over foreign productive assets through a variety of non-equity arrangements — subcontracting, franchising, licensing, and the like — as well as through the formation of strategic alliances. These forms of international expansion occur with little or no [foreign direct investment], and are therefore only partially captured by [foreign direct investment] data.

The significance of this is suggested by 'estimates ... that strategic alliances number in the thousands and subcontracting agreements alone in the hundreds of thousands' (ibid.). Unfortunately, data concerning transnationals' presence that take account of such forms of activity are not readily available.

In addition it is also important to appreciate that the data in Tables 2.1 and 2.2 focus on foreign investments; our concern is actually with the activities of all transnational corporations in an economy, not simply domestic firms operating overseas or overseas firms operating domestically. (The concern with all transnationals is not to deny that there may be important differences across firms within an economy but, as our analysis will show, for economies throughout the world problems arise as a result of the activities of all transnationals, whether domestic or overseas.) The significance of recognizing a broader concern with transnationals for an appreciation of transnationals' presence is enormous. This is suggested by estimates of transnationals' overall presence at a world level: it has been estimated that in 1988 the total value of the foreign direct capital stake of all transnationals was $1141 billion, equivalent to approximately 8 per cent of the combined gross domestic products of 'industrial market economies' and developing countries; the total value of these firms' foreign *and domestic* capital stake was approaching $5000 billion, approximately 35 per cent of the combined gross domestic products (Dunning 1993). In a similar vein, estimates suggest that in the mid-1980s transnationals 'were ... responsible for around three-quarters of the world's commodity trade, and four-fifths of the trade in technology and managerial skills' in the world's 'market economies' (ibid.).[1] (See also Dicken's 1992 discussion of the growth and spread of transnationals.)

As for evidence on particular nations, this is hard to come by. Nevertheless, Table 2.3 is of interest. It focuses on the United States and Japan. The data for Japan on foreign firms' influence may be thought to suggest that transnationals are unimportant in that economy (see also Table 2.2). In fact nothing could be further from the truth. In 1989 Japanese transnationals accounted for 37 per cent of total private firms' assets in Japanese manufacturing and 32 per cent

Table 2.3 The relative importance of transnationals in the USA and
Japan, 1989(%)

(i) USA: Share of transnationals in the assets and gross product of all
private firms

	US transnationals	Foreign transnationals	All transnationals
Assets	21.2	6.0	27.2
Gross product:			
Total[a]	26.2	5.7	31.9
Manufacturing	61.1	11.3	72.4

(ii) Japan: Share of transnationals in the assets and sales of all private firms[b]

	Japanese transnationals	Foreign transnationals[c]	All transnationals
Assets			
Total	23.6	0.9	24.5
Manufacturing	37.3	2.4	39.7
Sales			
Total	24.2	1.3	25.4
Manufacturing	32.1	2.8	34.9

[a] In these calculations, the figure for all private firms excludes banks.
[b] Excludes banking and insurance.
[c] Includes only majority owned affiliates.

Source: derived from United Nations (1993).

of their sales, figures which although very high are certain to be gross
underestimates because they focus on equity arrangements and
hence ignore the distinctive *keiretsu* networks that are such an important feature of the Japanese economy. As for the United States,
whereas foreign transnationals accounted for 6 per cent of total assets
of all private firms in the country and 6 per cent of their total gross
product, US transnationals accounted for a further 21 per cent and 26
per cent respectively. Furthermore, transnationals' influence over
manufacturing is especially important, to say the least; in all, transnationals accounted for over 72 per cent of private firms' gross product
in US manufacturing in 1989. Moreover, it is again worth stressing
that it is the giant transnationals that are especially significant.
Dunning (1993) reports the domestic and foreign assets of thirty-three
of the world's largest transnationals, twenty-two of these being US
firms. In 1989 these twenty-two had domestic assets of $1116 billion,
which amounted to 20.5 per cent of what United Nations (1993)
reports as the total assets of all private firms in the United States. This
compares in some sense to the 21.2 per cent figure reported in Table

2.3 for the share of all US transnationals in the total assets of all private firms in the United States. The comparison may be unreliable[2] but it is certainly clear that the twenty-two firms are extremely important.

Our conclusion is that the data point to giant transnationals as the major players in modern economies. The evidence we have presented is limited, as regards the particular impact of the largest firms and as regards its ability to capture the full extent of transnationals' activity, both in terms of ignoring the various ways influence can be exerted and in its focus on foreignness rather than the activities of transnationals as a whole. Nevertheless it is clear that a handful of the largest firms tend to dominate transnationals' activities, and it is beyond dispute that transnationals have a significant presence in the world's economies. It is against this background that we will now begin to characterize the nature and essence of these firms.

The nature and essence of the giant transnational

What is a transnational corporation?

An understanding of what is meant by the term transnational corporation has significant consequences for an understanding of the implications of transnationals' presence and should fundamentally shape the industrial economic strategies that countries and regions adopt. For this reason it is important to analyse the term in considerable depth.

Many researchers have put forward different definitions (see especially Aharoni's 1971 classification of suggestions on the basis of structural, performance and behavioural criteria). However, whilst many of these suggestions may be useful according to the particular points being analysed, to understand fully the nature and essence of the transnational corporation it is important to begin with the firm. After all, there is widespread consensus that a transnational is simply a firm which crosses national boundaries. Thus when thinking about transnationals we are forced into thinking about firms; hence there is an appealing logic to basing a definition on the theory of the firm.

Pursuing this logic, one possibility is to ground a definition in mainstream economic analysis, which on this issue to a large extent means returning to Coase's classic (1937) paper. Coase's starting point is that production is coordinated by the price mechanism (markets) and the task he sets himself is to explain why alternative means of coordination (firms) arise. His concern is to consider why firms exist 'in a specialised exchange economy in which it is generally assumed that the distribution of resources is "organised" by the price mechanism'. For him, the essence of the firm is that it is the means of coordinating production — seen as a set of transactions — without using market exchange. He argues that 'outside the firm ... production ... is coordinated through a series of exchange transactions on the market. Within a firm these market transactions are *eliminated*' (emphasis added). Hence a pure Coasian definition sees firms as the means of coordinating production without using market exchange. As for extending this analysis to the transnational corporation, following Buckley and Casson (1976), the pure Coasian approach sees a transnational as a firm in which the coordination of production without using market exchange takes the firm across national boundaries.

However, we take issue with this mainstream approach and prefer instead to develop an alternative. Our fundamental criticism is that it analyses from markets to firms and it focuses on market versus non-market activity. This focus is superficial and ignores what is really happening in production. Instead we suggest that a focus on strategic decision-making is more appropriate. For us, a firm is essentially about strategic decision-making. The consequences of a firm's presence are in many respects determined by the strategic decisions made within it, and in turn they depend crucially upon who is making the decisions. This is an argument which we will now begin to explain, explore and justify, although more detail on the theory of the firm can be found in Cowling and Sugden (1993a).

Mainstream economic analysis has become obsessed with markets and has failed to focus on what really happens when production takes place. In saying this we are joining with Aoki (1990a), Simon (1991) and even Coase (1991) in their recent criticisms of excessive concern in the theory of the firm with markets and exchanges. For example, Coase (1991) reflects that there has been 'an undue emphasis on the role of the firm as a purchaser of the services of the factors of production and on the choice of the contractual arrangements which it makes with them. As a consequence of this ... economists have tended to neglect the main activity of a firm, running a business'. This is a point taken up in Aoki (1990). Meanwhile for Simon (1991), classical and neoclassical theory, and the new institutional economics, put markets and exchanges centre stage. In contrast he suggests that 'the economics of modern industrialised society can *more appropriately* be labelled *organisational* economies than market economies' (emphasis added).

With such criticism in mind, the concern of a very extensive literature with firms' decision-making is particularly interesting. The
reason is that analyses of decision-making tend to concentrate directly
on what is actually happening when production takes place; they
tend to go to the heart of production, cutting through superficialities.
Such an incisive approach is precisely what we need for an alternative
analysis.

In general, the concern with decision-making is seen in such sem-
inal works as Simon (1959), arguing that satisficing is the norm, and
Cyert and March (1963), which develops an analysis closely associated
with all behavioural theories of the firm. Decision-making is also at
the heart of many contributions to the literature in the organizational
behaviour and management theory traditions. More specifically —
and for us more importantly — it is seen in analyses of the control of
firms.

Following Zeitlin (1974), control implies the ability to determine
broad corporate objectives despite resistance from others. In other
words, to control is to have the power to make decisions over
strategic issues — for example, concerning a firm's geographical orientation, and concerning its relationship with rivals, governments
and its labour force — and hence to take a firm in a particular direction even though others would prefer something different. This is not
to say that what actually happens in production is determined solely
by these strategic decisions. Rather, in a capitalist firm they are the
pinnacle of a hierarchical system of decision-making. They constrain
the operational, day-to-day decisions over such tactical issues as the
choice of a particular project from a subset of alternatives. Moreover
they also constrain the choices made by everybody in a firm over
work intensity, etc. Thus what actually happens in production is
determined by all three sets of decisions. Nevertheless it is the
strategic decisions which play the prime role because, by definition,
they determine a firm's broad direction (see Pitelis and Sugden 1986).

What all of this suggests is that the concept of strategic decision-
making goes to the core of the way in which production is carried
out. It implies that the crucial distinguishing feature of activities
within a firm is that they are subject to strategic decision-making from
one centre. Accordingly, based on this discussion we propose the following definition as an alternative to the pure Coasian approach: a
firm is the means of coordinating production from one centre of
strategic decision-making. Thus we see a transnational corporation as
the means of coordinating production from one centre of strategic

decision-making when this coordination takes a firm across national boundaries.

Perhaps a specific example from the real world will begin to provide better insight. Mitter (1986) describes the case of Benetton, a clothing producer with over 2500 shops world-wide. Benetton is reported as employing something less than 2000 people in 'its' eight factories in northern Italy and in addition as giving work to a further 6000 (also in northern Italy) employed by the 200 small subcontractors making semi-finished clothes which are supplied to the eight main plants. Mitter refers to the skilled parts of the production process — such as designing, cutting and final ironing — being 'handled by Benetton' whilst the basic weaving and making up is done 'outside the company's plant'. The reason: Benetton can thereby cut costs, for example, by benefiting from the lower costs of the small subcontractors. The boundaries Mitter draws around Benetton's operations are in line with the pure Coasian approach. In contrast, our view is that it is a priori artificial to separate Benetton's eight main plants from the 200 subcontractors. Rather, the transnational 'Benetton' should include market exchanges where they are coordinated from one centre of strategic decision-making — and Mitter at least leaves a strong suggestion that what she calls Benetton is indeed in control of its subcontractors, i.e. it does include the centre of strategic decision-making that encompasses the subcontractors' activities. Moreover the importance of this is suggested by the consequent difference in numbers of production workers employed by Benetton throughout northern Italy — 8000 rather than 2000, an increase of 300 per cent on Mitter's observation. Thus we suggest that the pure Coasian approach denies the especially important role of strategic decision-making in production, preferring a concern with superficial attributes that misrepresents the activities of firms and that can lead to misunderstanding and error.

Why does a firm produce in various countries?

Further insight can be achieved by deepening the analysis of the nature and essence of transnationals, more specifically by beginning to examine why a firm produces in more than one country. Moreover this deepening of the analysis begins to explore the impact of such firms, explicitly taken up in the next section.

Accepted theory on why firms produce in various countries has recently been dominated by Coasian analysis, more widely known as internalization or transactions costs analysis when it comes to this issue (see, for example, Hennart 1991 for a recent appreciation).

Following Coase's (1937) focus on market versus non-market exchange, a basic aspect of the internalization approach is to ask why production should entail non-market rather than market exchanges. The use of markets is seen as a benchmark, departures from which have to be explained. Moreover, the only contemplated basis for a departure is the incentive provided by the possibility of at least one person gaining and nobody losing: i.e. the only contemplated basis is a Pareto improvement. In its turn the basis for this Pareto criterion is the generally implicit assumption of voluntary exchange. The idea is that anybody and everybody has some sort of veto over outcomes that they find undesirable; if a change would make someone worse off, that someone would veto the change.

Thus the thrust of internalization analysis is that firms produce in various countries to bypass market exchanges and consequently save on transactions costs; the idea is to carry out a non-market transaction (i.e. exchange) rather than use a market. The emphasis is on at least somebody gaining and nobody losing. Potential losers from introducing a non-market transaction would veto the use of such a transaction, which they could not be forced to undertake; all transactions are entered into voluntarily. Furthermore, the fundamental source of gains is seen to be savings on transactions costs, a concept associated very much with Williamson (see especially Williamson 1975). The basic argument is that a transaction can be carried out by different means, each with a different cost, and that the transactors will take the least cost option.

Again, as with the definition problem, we take issue with this approach and prefer instead to develop an alternative framework. Analysis of what is meant by the term transnational and of why a firm is a transnational should fit together hand in glove. Hence it would be inconsistent for us to criticize pure Coasian definitions for analysing from markets to firms and for focusing on market versus non-market activity, yet not to criticize the parallel Coasian approach to why firms produce in various countries, when this also analyses from markets to firms and also focuses on market versus non-market activity. Again, we suggest it is inappropriate to ignore what is really happening in production. A focus on strategic decision-making is needed.

The decision on whether to produce in more than one country is a strategic decision which, by definition, will be made by a firm's strategic decision-makers despite resistance from others. Following our earlier characterization, the crucial feature of a typical capitalist firm is its hierarchical system of decision-making, with strategic decisions and therefore strategic decision-makers being at the pinnacle of the hierarchy. Precisely who a firm's strategic decision-makers are is the subject of controversy amongst economists. Some argue that they are senior managers, others that they are a subset of shareholders, others that these two groups are essentially the same set of people anyway (see, for instance, Cubbin and Leech 1983 on the proportion of shares needed for control). Our characterization of the firm is consistent with all of these views; hence it would be injecting unnecessary controversy into our analysis to choose between them. Recognizing this consistency is nevertheless important. In part, this is because such recognition goes some way to refuting the criticism that our analysis is burdened by a nineteenth-century view of the capitalist.[3] More positively, arguably the most important point in this debate on the control of firms is that all but the purest neo-classicists accept that strategic decision-makers are a subset of those involved with a capitalist firm and certainly do not include the general workforce. It thus follows that the decision on whether to produce in more than one country will be made by an élite, despite resistance from others.

The idea of making a decision despite resistance from others is only really meaningful if the decision-makers genuinely have a choice. For many economists, this would form a basis for criticizing our approach. The typical view in economics is that firms operate in a more or less perfectly competitive environment. For example, this is effectively true of pure Coasian analysis.[4] The typical view is sometimes relaxed after a while but usually as an appendix, with little thrust and, significantly, with competition still seen as the norm. If true, the view implies that strategic decision-makers will be forced by the competitive environment into the only course of action enabling the firm to avoid losses and continue in business. However, we suggest that in reality a firm's environment is typically not competitive. This is an argument that has been advanced in detail — both theoretically and empirically — by, in particular, monopoly capitalism analysis (see especially Baran and Sweezy 1966 and Cowling 1982). Furthermore, the argument has also received support from a wider literature.

One of the key theoretical points is that a firm will manipulate and shape its environment to ensure that the environment is not competitive. To illustrate, a view held by neo-classical economists is that if a firm is faced by a perfectly competitive product market, in the long run it would only ever achieve normal profits, just enough to keep it in business, no more and no less. The difficulty with arguing that such a situation is typical is that it flies in the face of all that a firm is attempting to accomplish, assuming it is a profit-seeker.[5] Clearly, then, a firm will attempt to avoid such competition; it will try to dominate its product market and, in the extreme, obtain pure monopoly profits. Part of the task a capitalist firm sets itself is therefore to develop ways of manipulating and shaping its product market — and indeed its environment more generally — to avoid competition. For instance, it may subvert technological change, withholding innovations to avoid disrupting an established monopoly position; it may create product market niches through appropriate marketing; it may seek exclusive access to raw materials; and it will collude with rivals. Furthermore, it is not simply the case that such courses of action give strategic decision-makers room for manœuvre; decisions over strategy will themselves be made with such concerns paramount. Suppose, for example, that a firm produces a particular good in country X and that it has to use a raw material exclusively mined in country Y. It may decide to take over the mine to ensure that rivals cannot obtain the raw material. In other words, to increase its product market power it may decide to produce in more than one country.

Moreover, empirical evidence for the idea that at least the strategic decision-makers of existing transnationals are not in fact constrained by perfectly competitive product markets seems to be clear. Thus Dunning (1993) concludes:

the widespread opinion held among scholars [is] that [transnationals'] attitudes are most pronounced in sectors where the market structure is best described as an amalgam of oligopolistic and monopolistic competition. In some sectors (eg oil, tobacco, aluminium, razor blades, rubber tyres and reinsurance) the output is largely in the hands of a few large firms. In others (eg cosmetics, pharmaceuticals, food processing, insurance and hotels) the concentration ratio is not as high, but the sector is characterised by other market imperfections (eg extensive product differentiation and entry barriers).

To explore and explain fully why firms produce in various countries would require a far more detailed appreciation of such theoretical and empirical evidence. However, it should already be becoming clear that our approach is very different to internalization analysis. Such production entails a strategic decision made by an élite despite opposition. What this implies is that a firm may decide to produce in various countries when others would wish it to do otherwise.[6] The reason it would produce in various countries is that this would suit the élite. As for the others who would prefer something different, they are not making the decision and therefore they essentially have no say. In other words, not everybody has a veto over outcomes they dislike. Thus when a firm decides to produce in various countries, the only certain thing is that those making the decision will gain (unless they have made a mistake) whilst others may lose.

Key features of giant transnational corporations: a recap

Our aim has been to focus on the nature and essence of the typical giant transnational. To do this we have considered what is meant by the term transnational corporation and then gone on to examine why a firm chooses to produce in various countries. We will be returning to the latter with more detailed arguments subsequently in the volume; until now our explicit intention has only ever been to begin to examine the issue.

We have not yet identified every important feature of the giant transnational. However, we suggest that our analysis thus far has revealed some crucial and quite general characteristics of these firms: they are centres of strategic decision-making; they are a means for an élite to make strategic decisions despite the resistance of others; they enable an élite to pursue their objectives whilst others with an interest in production are excluded; when a strategic decision is made by a transnational the only certain thing is that it will benefit an élite (assuming that élite has not made a mistake) whilst others may lose.

The consequences of giant transnationals' presence: market power in product markets

The characteristics of giant transnationals that we have highlighted lead us to conclude that the economies dominated by these firms are subject to systemic deficiencies. Such economies are inflicted with inherent problems and thus fail society. This is an indictment we will explore and explain in some detail in this and the following three chapters. Our discussion now will focus on product market monopolization.

A tendency towards product market monopolization has significant consequences for the well-being of communities. Mainstream literature focuses in particular on its implications for allocative inefficiency, especially dead-weight loss (the reduced consumer and producer surplus resulting from monopoly rather than perfectly competitive pricing), and X-inefficiency (associated with the greater costs implied by monopoly rather than perfectly competitive production) (see Scherer and Ross 1990). Moreover the monopoly capitalism literature particularly emphasizes the consequences for income distribution, an aspect of people's well-being that is crucial but one that is often neglected by economists. To illustrate, consider an industry's price-marginal cost margin, also known as its degree of monopoly; a higher margin implies that an industry is closer to the pure monopoly position whilst perfect competition implies a margin of zero, i.e. a zero degree of monopoly. Following the pioneering work of Kalecki (1971), if firms are assumed to face constant marginal costs the share of industry wages in value added depends upon the degree of monopoly and the ratio of the industry wages bill to its raw materials expenditure. More specifically, if the wages bill:raw materials expenditure ratio is constant, a rise in an industry's degree of monopoly must be accompanied by a fall in the share of value added going to wages. Similarly, a *ceteris paribus* rise in an industry's degree of monopoly must be accompanied by a rise in the share of value added going to 'gross capitalist income and salaries' (i.e. profit, interest, rent, depreciation and salaries). This is shown in detail by Cowling (1982), where the fixed marginal cost assumption is justified as realistic.[7] Put more loosely, an increase in an industry's degree of monopoly tends to be associated with a fall of the wage share and a rise of the profit share in the industry.

To assess the impact of giant transnationals on market power we will consider their impact on an industry's degree of monopoly. This is an obvious step, bearing in mind the crucial relationship between the degree of monopoly and income distribution that we have just outlined, and given that the degree of monopoly (i.e. the price-marginal cost margin) is clearly a more general measure of the extent of monopoly and hence of market power effects more widely. Unfortunately, it is also a step which cannot draw on a wide existing literature, where the subject has been given scant attention and where the focus has been on other measures of market power (see, for instance, Dunning 1993). Accordingly we will first of all discuss the determinants of the degree of monopoly in general. This will entail a consideration of pricing behaviour. We will then explore the impact of giant transnationals.

Our basic argument will be that an industry's degree of monopoly depends fundamentally on firms' retaliatory power; specifically, what is crucial is firms' ability to detect and respond to each other's attempts to gain at rivals' expense. Furthermore we will suggest that firms' retaliatory power will tend to be greater when the industry is characterized by the presence of giant transnationals. Putting these two points together, we will argue that market power in the product market may be more of a problem in capitalist economies because of the presence of giant transnationals.

The determinants of an industry's degree of monopoly

An industry's degree of monopoly is an aspect of industry performance. To begin to explore its determinants we draw on the structure/conduct/performance paradigm. This is a line of reasoning that goes back to the 1930s. Within this paradigm, whilst it is argued that there is not a unidirectional causal relationship between structure, conduct and performance, there is seen to be a strong causal link running from industry conduct to industry performance. The idea of expecting conduct, i.e. behaviour, essentially to determine performance is something we find very plausible and is therefore the starting point for our analysis. The particular aspect of performance we are concerned with is the degree of monopoly and thus our initial task is to highlight the crucial aspects of firms' behaviour that will determine performance on this issue.

To do this we begin with Stigler's (1968) observation that a firm's behaviour is something to be deduced from its objectives. Thus assuming that the élite strategic decision-makers desire maximum profits, then 'profit-maximising must imply the form of [firm] behaviour — economic behaviour is a means to achieve this end, not a separate part of man to be supplied by a psychiatrist or a sociologist' (Stigler 1968). With this in mind we suggest that a crucial determinant of firms' performance is collusion over prices amongst those firms. The reason for this is that it is *because* strategic decision-makers in capitalist firms seek profits that firms will collude over prices. This may not suit others in society but they are not setting firms' objectives, hence determining firms' basic behaviour; if they were, they would be strategic decision-makers.

The idea of collusion because firms seek profits is recognized by Scherer, amongst others: 'when the number of sellers is small, each firm recognises that aggressive action such as price-cutting will induce counter-action from rivals which, in the end, leave all members of the industry worse off. All may therefore exercise mutual restraint and prevent prices falling to the competitive level' (Scherer 1980). Baran and Sweezy take a similar view (1966):

the typical giant corporation ... is one of several corporations producing commodities which are more or less adequate substitutes for each other. When one of them varies its price, the effect will be felt by the others. If firm A lowers its price, some new demand will be tapped, but the main effect will be to attract customers away from firms B, C and D. The latter, not willing to give up their business to A, will retaliate by lowering their prices, perhaps even undercutting A. While A's original move was made in the expectation of increasing its profit, the net result may be to leave all the firms in a worse position ... Unstable market situations of this sort ... are anathema to the big corporations ... To avoid such situations therefore becomes the first concern of corporate policy.

The crucial basic principle is that no firm will act in a way which leaves itself worse off, bearing in mind the retaliation of rivals. Thus collusion amongst firms is simply the avoidance of pricing behaviour which leaves each and every firm worse off and it derives from recognition of the 'retaliatory' power of rivals. Whilst, if circumstances allowed, a firm would not hesitate to become a pure monopolist by driving rivals from the industry, more generally it cannot do this and will therefore accommodate their presence. Likewise a firm will appreciate that rivals tolerate its presence because of its retaliatory power.

Some may object to use of the term collusion to depict conduct that is simply avoiding situations which leave all firms worse off. Some may like to think of collusion as necessarily involving a conspiracy hatched behind closed doors in a secret, smoke-filled room. However, the sort of behaviour we are depicting clearly is a conspiracy; it essentially entails a set of élite strategic decision-makers furthering their objectives by refraining from mutually disadvantageous activity. It may or may not entail secret meetings in smoke-filled rooms but that is essentially a trivial irrelevance; a conspiracy requires communication between the conspirators but that does not even require talking, let alone secret meetings. More importantly, it also ought to be recognized that many authors define collusion differently. For example, Waterson (1984) takes the typical view that collusion refers to implicit or explicit joint profit maximization amongst firms.

We suggest that joint profit maximization may or may not be the outcome of collusion. However, it is certainly relevant to our analysis. Indeed, there is a sense in which the polar case of ultimate success for strategic decision-makers in colluding capitalist firms is joint profit maximization. This follows from the assumption that capitalist firms seek profits and from the point that collectively profits can never be higher than at the joint maximum. As Baran and Sweezy (1966) comment, 'sellers of a given commodity or of close substitutes have an interest in seeing that the price or prices established are such as to maximise the profits of the group as a whole'. Nevertheless we are not suggesting that colluders will necessarily be totally successful in this sense.

To the extent that they are not, the reason must be because at least one firm (believes it) is better off away from joint maximization; if this is not the case they are all worse off and they would collude to avoid such an outcome.[8] It is thus vital to explore why a firm may believe it is better off not maximizing joint profits. We suggest that the reason is to be found in the concept of retaliatory power. To explain, it has been argued that firms collude over prices because of their retaliatory power. However, there is no a priori reason to expect the retaliatory power of firms in one industry to be the same as the retaliatory power of firms in another industry in all circumstances. Suppose, for instance, that at a particular point the retaliatory power of firms in industry A is very low and in industry B is very high. In either case, if a firm cuts its price rivals will retaliate, but in industry A the retaliation may take so long to come and may be so weak when it does come that it does not deter the price cut. In short, the potential price cutter in industry A may calculate that the retaliation of rivals would not leave it worse off, in which case it will indeed cut price. In contrast, the potential price-cutter in B is faced with rivals with higher retaliatory power, perhaps so high that it expects any attempted price cut would leave it worse off. Hence it will not cut price.

To give this argument more substance, consider another simple example (building on the discussion of exchange rate adjustment and oligopoly pricing behaviour in Cowling and Sugden 1989). Suppose firm i was to cut its price. The consequent change in its profits would depend crucially upon when rivals respond and the strength of that response. Generally response would not be immediate because it takes time both to detect cuts and to formulate the desired response. Thus initially the price cut would generally yield i increased profits as it would give i the new buyers that are attracted to the industry and the new buyers attracted from rivals. But when rivals do respond, they would cut their prices in an attempt to attract back buyers from firm i and thereby re-establish profits.[9] As a consequence firm i's profits would fall. Whether or not firm i would cut its price in the first place depends upon whether or not rivals have the power to turn the effects of i's price cut into overall losses for i. Moreover, what is especially important in this calculation is what may be termed rivals' detection power and rivals' response power. Detection power refers to the ability to identify a price cut and formulate a response. The greater rivals' detection power, other things being equal, the less likely is i to find a price cut attractive. As for response power, it refers to rivals' ability to push down i's profits. The greater rivals' response power, the less likely is i to find a price cut attractive, other things being equal.

Thus we have suggested that (1) profit-seeking implies collusive pricing behaviour by oligopolists and by giant firms, and (2) there is a sense in which ultimate success for colluding capitalist firms is joint profit maximization, but (3) variations across industries in firms' retaliatory power — especially their detection power and response power — explain why some industries may not reach this high point. Bearing in mind that a central thrust of the monopoly capitalism literature is that industries in general are typically oligopolies where giant firms dominate, what we can conclude is that the case of pure monopoly provides a sensible benchmark for analysing industry pricing, and that deviations from this benchmark are caused by industry variations in the retaliatory power of firms. (This is clearly very different from the typical economists' argument, where the benchmark tends to be perfect competition.) Put another way, pricing in an industry depends crucially upon the retaliatory power of its firms; the greater the retaliatory power of the firms, the less likely is the industry to deviate from behaving as if it were a pure monopoly.

This has crucial implications for industry performance. The particular aspect of industry performance that we are focusing upon here is its price-marginal cost margin, i.e. its so-called degree of monopoly. What our conclusion implies for this is that an industry's degree of monopoly depends fundamentally upon firms' retaliatory power. A standard result in price theory is that the price-marginal cost margin in a pure monopoly is given by $1/\epsilon$, where ϵ is the (absolute value of the) industry's price elasticity of demand. Thus what we are suggesting is that, in so far as an industry's price-marginal cost margin is in fact less than $1/\epsilon$, the cause is to be found in the retaliatory power of its firms. Moreover, in so far as such deviation varies over time, the explanation is found in alterations in firms' retaliatory power. Turning this around, if there is reason to believe that the retaliatory power of an industry's firms has increased (decreased) over time, it is possible that its degree of monopoly has also increased (decreased). This is not to say that a change in the degree of monopoly is certain because, for example, the retaliatory power of firms may differ between two points in time yet on both occasions may be sufficient to keep the industry performing as if it were a pure monopoly. Nevertheless, it is a possibility, and it is with this in mind that the presence of giant transnationals is important.

Giant transnationals and the degree of monopoly

The significance of giant transnational corporations is that they tend to have very high retaliatory power, higher than other firms. Hence if an industry is not maximizing joint profits before transnationals become major players, it may be doing so once they have emerged; it is certainly the case that transnationals' presence is likely to push the degree of monopoly higher.

There are various reasons for transnationals having high retaliatory power. Not least amongst these reasons, the very explanation for a firm's strategic decision-makers opting for production in various countries may be to enhance or maintain its retaliatory power. Consider a scenario based on the view developed in Knickerbocker (1973) and also discussed by Vernon (1977) in the context of car, consumer electronics and tyre production in Latin America and Asia. Suppose two rival firms, i and j, initially supply country X from factories overseas but that j becomes a transnational by establishing production facilities inside X. Firm i may see j's move as posing important risks to its profits: perhaps j will be able to take advantage of lower production costs in X to undercut massively firm i's price, and hence undermine i's profits. Faced with this, i may decide to match its rival and also become a transnational. Its ultimate aim is to maintain its profits but to do so it seeks to maintain its retaliatory power.

Moreover, transnationals' detection power is likely to be relatively strong. Detection refers to a firm's ability to identify changes in rivals' activities and to formulate a response. It not only requires the interpretation of information, but also its collection and its being made available to decision-makers. Good internal communication is therefore vital to a firm. An advantage of transnationals in this respect is their appreciation of and experience with modern communication techniques, including methods of organizing the firm. This is well documented. Hymer (1972), for instance, refers to the importance of organizational form and Vernon (1977) feels that 'the international telephone, the computer and the commercial aircraft have been indispensable to the growth of such enterprises'. Similarly, Barnet and Muller (1974) emphasize the importance of information flows in such firms.

Superior detection power is also implied by the special significance for at least some transnationals of inter-firm collaborative ventures (which is not to say that this is necessarily a prime reason why collaboration has occurred). The world motor vehicles industry is a good case in point; Dicken (1992) reports a maze of inter-firm agreements involving transnationals. He tells of the collaboration between General Motors and Toyota to build a small car in the United States and of a similar relationship between Chrysler and Mitsubishi; of the 'exceptionally complex network of relationships between the major automobile manufacturers' in Japan, including collaboration between Mazda and Ford, Nissan and Volkswagen; and he reports that in Europe 'virtually all the major European manufacturers are involved in collaborative deals'. Dicken (1992) also reports collaboration in consumer electronics, for example, between Philips and Sony in developing compact disc technology, and in semi-conductors (and see also United Nations 1993 on telecommunications, biotechnology, chemicals, foodstuffs and other industries). The importance of such collaboration to detection power is that generally collaborative ventures will enable firms to understand each other all the better. For instance, working together can only help the understanding between General Motors, Toyota, Nissan, Volkswagen and the other motor manufacturers. The result is that transnationals will build a better picture of which rivals might be more likely to indulge in price-cutting and hence which require close scrutiny. It could be, for example, that certain firms are persistent offenders; for some reason or another they have a tendency to attempt to gain profits at rivals' expense by cutting price.

Greater understanding between firms will also tend to follow from their being rivals in different situations. This is similar to the case of people: more contact is inclined to lead to more knowledge and understanding. And again transnationals are especially significant in this respect, because their global activities bring them into contact with each other in different countries.[10] Moreover, another effect of contact in different situations is that it is likely to increase transnationals' response power. This refers to a firm's ability adversely to affect rivals' profits. Edwards (1955, 1979) argues that when firms have reiterated contacts with each other, faced with a problem in one situation they will decide what to do by bearing in mind their relationship more widely. A number of writers have been concerned with this in the context of a particular country (see, for example, the empirical analysis of the United States in Feinberg 1985, but it is clearly very relevant to transnationals. Suppose, for example, transnationals i and j produce and sell a particular good in countries X, Y and Z. If firm i contemplates any price-cutting in country X, retaliation from firm j could come from any or all of the countries. One possibility is for j to increase its output in all three, another to use production from Y, and Z to swamp country X with vastly increased sales, always assuming some freedom of international trade that permits this to happen. In short, then, transnationals have the ability to respond from and in all or some of the countries in which they operate. This can only imply higher response power compared to other firms.

More generally, transnationals can respond using all of their global resources. For instance, they can finance response in one country by profits from elsewhere, which is undoubtedly important because retaliation by cutting price not only requires that more is produced but also that it is produced without bankruptcy. Of course, any firm can draw on all of its resources but a distinguishing feature of giant transnationals is their sheer size. This is again well evidenced. For example, Benson and Lloyd (1983) have observed that of the 100 largest economic units in the world, only half are nation states; the other half are transnationals! Suffice it to say that for other firms, the wrath of such giants would be overwhelming.

This and our other reasons for suggesting that transnationals have comparatively high retaliatory power imply that the precise extent of their influence depends upon various factors. Nevertheless, the especially important implication is that where giant transnationals have a significant presence in an industry, product market monopolization may be more of a problem; if the industry price-marginal cost margin was not at the pure monopoly level before transnationals became prominent, it may have become so, and certainly it is likely to have been pushed higher.

Thus we have shown that the presence of giant transnational corporations implies systemic problems associated with product market monopolization. The implications for allocative inefficiency and functional income distribution are issues that communities faced by transnationals need to take into account; they are implications that go to the heart of community well-being. However, it must also be emphasized that this is only the beginning of the problem of transnationalism. Other consequences focus on: tendencies to centripetalism and short-termism, as well as subversion of international trade; divide and rule of labour and governments; deindustrialization and demand-side stagnation. It is to these issues that we now turn in the following three chapters.

Notes

1 These figures, like all other data in this section, ignore non-equity arrangements. Hence, as Dunning (1993) recognizes, they are underestimates.

2 It is not clear that assets in Dunning (1993) are defined in the same way as assets in United Nations (1993).

3 Some have seen our analysis as burdened by an outdated image of strategic decision-makers as nineteenth-century factory owners. This is partly refuted by the fact that the analysis accommodates these different views on who controls *today's* firms. Moreover we would also argue that the forebears of today's capitalist organizations are in fact nineteenth-century capitalist organizations, with which there is indeed considerable underlying similarity (see Hymer 1972 on the evolution of transnationals from Marshallian type firms, and Pitelis and Sugden's 1986 theoretical treatment of the control issue).

4 It focuses on the replacement of imperfect market exchanges with non-market exchanges yielding the perfectly competitive outcome of Pareto efficiency (a situation where nobody can be made better off without making someone worse off).

5 This assumption is quite general in the sense that it is consistent with various views on who makes strategic decisions, be it managers, some or even all shareholders. There is detailed discussion in Cowling (1982) of the consistency between profit maximization and managerialism, reflected in intra-corporate consumption out of non-reported profits. More generally on strategic decision-making and firms' objectives, see Pitelis and Sugden (1986).

6 We are implicitly assuming that strategic decision-makers in capitalist economies pursue selfish interests. At least amongst economists this should cause no queries; such an assumption lies at the heart of much, indeed most economic analysis.

7 More formally, denote the industry degree of monopoly as μ, industry profits as π, industry fixed costs as F and industry total revenue as T. Then $\mu = (\pi + F)/T$. Assume costs comprise only raw material and wage bills, and denote industry value added as Y, where $Y = \pi + F + W$, total wages being W. Then, by substituting into the expression for μ and rearranging:

$$\frac{W}{Y} = 1 - \mu \frac{T}{y} \qquad \text{and} \qquad \frac{(\pi + F)}{Y} = \mu \frac{T}{Y}$$

Cowling (1982) explains that an alteration in T/Y is the same as an alteration in the ratio of the industry's wages bill to its raw materials expenditure. See also Cowling and Molho (1982).

8 We are ignoring the possibility of being neither worse off nor better off.

9 Because firm i's price cut would attract buyers from rivals, rivals' profits must decline for as long as they make no response.

10 For instance, Dicken (1986) reports evidence on the geographical distribution of foreign affiliates of nearly 10,000 transnationals in 1973. Over 30 per cent had affiliates in more than five countries. Moreover, the gloss on this general picture is that amongst the largest transnationals the dispersion is even greater. For example, in 1950 approximately one-quarter of the largest 180 US transnationals operated in over five countries but by 1975 this had risen to very nearly all (see Vernon 1979).

3

THE INTERNATIONAL ECONOMIC
SYSTEM

We have characterized the nature and essence of the giant transnational corporation as a centre of strategic decision-making, a means
for an élite to make strategic decisions in the pursuit of their interests
despite the resistance of others. These firms have been depicted as the
major players in today's world economy. Our aim now is to focus
directly on the international economic system *per se* — as against its
constituent parts, or more particularly its major players — and thus to
consider some further consequences of these major players having a
significant presence.

   We will first of all depict the nature and essence of the international
economic system. This will entail further, relatively detailed discussion of transnationals *per se* but our particular concern is to examine
the system as a whole. The analysis will draw on Hymer's (1972) path-
breaking vision of the world economy, essentially arguing that the
structure and organization of the international economy will mirror
the structure and organization of giant transnationals. We will suggest that the international economic system is characterized by firms
with a more or less global spread but whose strategic decision-making
is confined to a handful of locations. This implies that, taking the
system as a whole, production activities are more or less spread
throughout the world according to the relative attraction of particular
locations for achieving the objectives of firms' strategic decision-
makers, but that strategic decision-making itself is very highly concentrated. We will then explore this by considering the variation in
structure and organization across different transnationals. This will
lead us to highlight some further consequences of transnationals'

presence: the subversion of international trade, centripetalism and short-termism.

The argument about international trade will essentially be that transnationals want so-called free international trade, i.e. trade free from interference by particular nations, so that they can manage trade in their own interests. We will be suggesting that an international economic system with free international trade is in fact a system of transnationals' subverted trade. As regards centripetalism, it will be argued that there is a tendency for higher-level economic, political and social activities to gravitate to the centre, away from the periphery. Transnationals' strategic decision-making is concentrated in a handful of major cities in the world, with far-reaching consequences for particular nations and communities; a nation's pattern of development depends crucially upon its position in the world order, yet that position is essentially determined by firms' strategic decision-makers, not by the citizens of the nation as such. Related to this, it will also be argued that there is a tendency for particular communities to be unable to pursue their long-run development, with which they may be especially concerned. The basic difficulty is again that the strategic decision-making of firms is based on the wishes of an élite, not communities; hence whilst transnationals might plan long-term, this is by no stretch of the imagination long-term planning by the communities in which they do or do not operate.

The nature and essence of the international economic system

Geographically concentrated strategic decision-making

It was argued by Stephen Hymer more than twenty years ago that if giant transnational corporations dominate the world economy, the structure and organization of such firms will be reflected in the structure and organization of the international economic system. His is a vision which has since been criticized on its details (see, for example, Dicken 1992), but one which we find extremely relevant in its overall thrust and in its applicability to the 1990s.

Hymer (1972) focuses on various levels of managerial decision-making in the typical firm, arguing in particular that whereas some activities in transnationals would be spread throughout the world 'according to the pull of manpower, markets and raw materials', top management would tend to be geographically very concentrated. His basic idea is that firms are characterized by a vertical division of labour, for example, the top level of management being concerned with goal determination and planning whereas the lowest level is concerned with managing day-to-day events within an established framework. Hymer (ibid.) argues that this lowest level would be widely spread in a giant transnational; thus, for example, it might be supervising unskilled production, which might be carried out in various parts of the world, wherever unskilled labour is cheaply available. By contrast, he suggested that top management in a transnational

must be located close to the capital market, the media and the government. Nearly every major corporation in the United States, for example, must have its general office (or a large portion of its high-level personnel) in or near the city of New York, because of the need for face-to-face contact at higher levels of decision making.

The crucial implication that Hymer draws from this for the international economic system is that there would be 'a hierarchical division of labour between geographical regions corresponding to the vertical division of labour within the firm'. He concludes:

one would expect to find the highest offices of the [transnational corporations] concentrated in the world's major cities ... These ... will be the major centres of high-level strategic planning. Lesser cities throughout the world will deal with the day-to-day operations of specific local problems. These in turn will be arranged in a hierarchical fashion: the larger and more important ones will contain regional corporate headquarters while the smaller ones will be confined to lower level activities.

He also argues that, as a consequence of their status and authority, the major centres would attract the best and most highly paid doctors, lawyers, educators, actors, hairdressers, and so on; the structure of income and consumption across the world would reflect the corporate hierarchy; the citizens of the major cities would receive the greatest income and, because they have more money to experiment with, would be the first to experience new consumption goods. Thus, in the international economic system:

income, status, authority, and consumption patterns would radiate out from [the major] centres along a declining curve, and the existing patterns of inequality and dependency would be perpetuated. The pattern would be complex, just as the structure of the corporation is complex, but the basic relationship between different countries would be one of superior and subordinate, head office and branch plant.

Despite criticism of Hymer's (1972) analysis for over-simplifying a complex reality, it was intended as a characterization and as such his arguments have considerable appeal. As Dicken (1992) concludes:

there *are* recognisable hierarchical spatial tendencies in the location of different parts of transnationals. Corporate headquarters *do* tend to concentrate in a small number of metropolitan centres; regional offices *do* favour a slightly wider range of cities; production units *are* more extensively spread both within and between nations, in developed and developing countries.

It seems that there is indeed a correspondence principle relating the structure and organization of transnational corporations to the structure and organization of the international economic system.

We suggest that in fact an international economic system dominated by giant transnational corporations is simultaneously subjected to both centrifugal and centripetal tendencies (see Cowling 1991). The centrifugal tendency can be seen most clearly in the case of unskilled activities. These know few geographical bounds; this is precisely because they are unskilled and can therefore be performed by workers in most parts of the world. But the same principle holds more generally. Thus within Europe, for instance, the emergence of transnational corporations has contributed to more and more of the continent being opened up to more and more manufacturing and indeed other activities. With the European Union's Single Market initiatives and the erosion of the Iron Curtain, we can expect to see a continuing movement of production from the older industrialized economies of North-West Europe to the less developed economies of the Mediterranean Rim and to the transition economies of Eastern Europe. This is because location of some activity in the Mediterranean Rim and Eastern Europe can sometimes offer transnationals better opportunities to pursue their objectives. With no trade barriers, for example, there may be nothing to prevent a giant transnational shipping components to Spain or Portugal for assembly by cheap and unskilled labour, and then shipping finished goods to markets throughout the European Union. Moreover, within this movement to the Mediterranean and the East we can also expect important qualitative differences, according to the relative attributes of particular locations *vis-à-vis* the particular requirements of transnational corporations, or more specifically (and in line with Chapter 2), the requirements of strategic decision-makers in transnationals. Hence we might expect, say, former East Germany to receive production activity requiring a higher skill content than, say, Portugal or Romania. This is a view supported by CEPR (1990), which concludes that the level of human capital is significantly higher in Eastern Europe than in Greece, Portugal and Spain. More generally, this European example points to a strong centrifugal tendency within the international economic system as a whole; production activity moves from core to periphery in the course of economic development as and when barriers to such movement are eroded.

Simultaneously, however, there is also an extremely important centripetal tendency. This concerns the location of strategic decision-making. It is important to recognize that any shift in production activity in a world dominated by transnational corporations does not imply a relocation of strategic decision-making. Other than with the peculiar circumstances surrounding a renaissant Berlin, there is no reason for strategic decision-makers to abandon their present locations, let alone spread themselves to a large number of dispersed, new locations. A mere handful of cities like New York, Tokyo, Frankfurt, Paris and London will remain the key cities of the world. Indeed, their joint dominance will grow with the growth in dominance of the transnationals whose headquarters they contain.

In short, then, the international economic system is characterized by firms with a more or less global spread but firms where strategic decisions are made in a handful of locations. Taking the system as a whole, whilst production activities are more or less spread throughout the world according to the relative attraction of particular locations for achieving the objectives of firms' strategic decision-makers, strategic decision-making itself is very highly concentrated.

Variation in transnationals' structure and organization

To explore this characterization in greater detail, it is useful to consider the variation in structure and organization in different transnationals, if only to pre-empt the criticism that the characterization is too simplistic for an admittedly complex world. Some may feel that variation across firms makes our characterization of the typical giant transnational, hence of the international economic system, suspect. To do this we will draw on the very recent discussion of transnationals' structure and organization in United Nations (1993) and then focus on the argument that many firms have been recently reorganizing themselves along lines reminiscent of the characteristics of flexible specialization (see Sabel 1988).

United Nations (1993) argues that the range of corporate strategies and hence structures of transnationals has increased over time, and that recently there has been a tendency among transnationals in many industries towards greater integration of their cross-national activities. It discusses separately the different ways that transnationals organize themselves functionally and the different ways that they organize themselves geographically, although these two issues are clearly related. We will now consider each of these in turn.

As regards corporate strategies over the organization of different functions in a firm, they are said to range from the organization of overseas production by so-called 'stand-alone affiliates' that carry out many functions for themselves, to 'complex integration strategies' where 'any affiliate operating anywhere may perform either by itself or with other affiliates or the parent firm, functions for the firm as a whole'. However, we suggest that in all instances what is crucial is that the function of strategic decision-making tends to remain central-ized at the firm's home base. With the stand-alone strategy, for example, United Nations (1993) recognizes that affiliates 'operate *largely* as independent concerns within the host economy' and that 'the main link between a parent and its foreign affiliates is *control* through ownership' (our emphasis). With the complex strategies, strategic decision-making also tends to remain centralized at the firm's home base and other functions are located wherever they best serve the firm's overall objective. According to the United Nations, 'a firm's ability to shift production or supply to wherever it is most prof-itable' is a key to understanding this location decision; in other words, it is important to appreciate that strategic decision-makers will ensure that production activity is located in whatever country a firm can obtain the highest profits. What this means in practice is that, at the firm level, the complex integration strategies simultaneously imply centralizing and decentralizing tendencies. The decentralizing ten-dency can be seen in the relocation of functions which have previ-ously been concentrated at a transnational's home base. Thus United Nations (1993) reports:

a growing number of [transnationals] have been locating a small (but rising) portion of their research and development activities outside their home country. One reason is to take advantage of the skills available abroad. For example, the research by IBM on high temperature super-conductivity was done in Switzerland. The growing importance of research and development has also led to more of it being located near factories and near markets. The big Japanese automobile producers, for example, do some of their research and development in the United States, where they have begun to design models for world-wide sales. Ford has taken this kind of integration a step further with its Mondeo model, assembling a research, development and design team headed by Ford of Europe and linked to numerous sites in Europe and North America via computer-communication networks.

On the other hand, a centralizing tendency at the firm level is seen by examples of transnationals concentrating a particular function in one location — not necessarily the home base — rather than leaving stand-alone affiliates to each carry out the function for themselves. This tendency can be seen in areas such as accounting and procurement. For example, United Nations (1993) reports the decision by ITT, a US firm that produces 'yellow-pages' business directories in various countries, to centralize the procurement of paper for its world-wide activities in a Belgian affiliate. Similarly, it reports that Swissair has transferred its revenue accounting work from local branches in various countries to an affiliate in India.

According to United Nations (1993), an implication of using such complex integration strategies is that some firms are establishing so-called 'functional headquarters' away from their overall head office. Its discussion of this point suggests unambiguously that strategic decision-making in transnationals characterized by complex integration strategies is very much the preserve of a centralized core group. Thus it observes:

corporate units in charge of a particular function — which might be termed 'functional headquarters' — are responsible for a specific activity for a [transnational] ... An international procurement office, an affiliate that coordinates sales and marketing internationally or an affiliate in charge of after-sales services, are examples of functional headquarters ... Establishing functional headquarters outside the home country for particular functions reduces the scope of responsibility that the headquarters at home assumes and *allows it to focus on the overall coordination of the various dispersed functions, while retaining some key functions, such as strategic planning* or finance. In turn, each headquarters in charge of a specific function ... bears the responsibility for performing that function and *reports directly to the top level of management in the home country.* (emphasis added)

All of this discussion is in line with our basic characterization of the international economic system. It is clearly consistent with the view that firms' strategic decisions are made in a handful of locations: we have simply suggested that the various corporate strategies for organizing functional activities are scenarios where the strategic decision-making function tends itself to remain centralized at the firm's home base. That the discussion implies strategic decision-making concentrated in a handful of locations follows from the fact that the home base of transnationals, and certainly the giants, tends to be in the so-called triad of the United States, Japan and the European Union. This is clear from the evidence presented by United Nations (1993): for example, of the 100 largest non-financial transnational corporations (ranked by foreign assets) in 1990, eighty-two had their home base in the triad (the others being from Switzerland (six), Sweden (five), Canada (three), Australia (two), New Zealand (one) and Norway (one)). It is for this reason that a handful of cities like New York, Tokyo, Frankfurt, Paris and London are the key cities of the international economic system. In line with this, Feagin and Smith (1987) report that in 1984 New York had the headquarters of fifty-nine of the top 500 transnationals (excluding banks), London had thirty-seven, Tokyo thirty-four, Paris twenty-six. All cities with five or more of the top 500 were in the United States, Japan, Britain, France, Germany, Italy, Canada and Sweden. Korea was the only Third World country with a city containing the headquarters of two or more top transnationals; Seoul had four. Clearly most top transnationals are headquartered in large cities, but many large cities do not have significant concentrations of this sort of international economic power. The cities of Mexico City, São Paulo, Calcutta, Buenos Aires, Bombay, Peking, Rio de Janeiro, Cairo and Shanghai do not figure in this respect.

Furthermore, our discussion of United Nations (1993) is also consistent with the view that the emergence of transnational corporations has contributed to more and more of the world being opened up to more and more manufacturing and indeed other activities. United Nations (1993) observes a tendency towards more complex integration strategies amongst transnationals. In so far as this implies more functions being transferred from the home base, it suggests more activities being opened to so-called host countries. In so far as it implies more functions being concentrated in one place, it implies that the input required by a transnational from any one affiliate is more specialized. This opens more of the world to more activities because those countries limited to performing particular functions can slot more easily into a transnational's operations.

Turning now from the ways transnationals organize themselves functionally to the ways they organize themselves geographically, United Nations (1993) again focuses on a range of possibilities. For example, it identifies 'multi-country strategies', where a transnational includes several affiliates, each primarily serving its host country. It also identifies 'regional strategies', where the transnational separates its production and selling activities along regional lines and, within each region, establishes an integrated production system which spans various countries. These possibilities relate to the various scenarios for organizing different functions within a firm. The idea seems to be that the multi-country strategy fits in with the use of stand-alone affiliates, whereas regional strategies are associated with more complex integration schemes. The United Nations view seems to be that regional strategies are emerging as especially important. It notes:

in recent years technological advances in transport and communications have reduced the costs of cross-national coordination. As trade barriers have been reduced and regional economic groupings formed, some [transnationals] have turned affiliates that previously served single countries into part of a more integrated production network to serve a larger market. That has occurred within the European Community as part of the transition to the Single Market. It has also happened in the four-nation Southern Cone Common Market — Argentina, Brazil, Paraguay and Uruguay — in Latin America: Ford (United States) and Volkswagen (Germany) are two examples. Transnational corporations are integrating affiliates in Mexico into a North American production network, in anticipation of a North American Free Trade Area.

Again, however, the variation in the ways that transnationals organize their activities is in line with our basic depiction of the international economic system. Both multi-country strategies and regional strategies are consistent with the view that firms' strategic decisions are made in a handful of locations. United Nations (1993) makes this very clear as regards the former; it suggests that, in a multi-country strategy, 'an affiliate primarily serves the host country market while the parent [transnational] *controls* several affiliates in different countries' (our emphasis). In other words, strategic decision-making remains with the so-called parent. But also in the case of regional strategies, it is strategic decision-makers who establish a structure where production is coordinated across a region, and where all regions essentially report back and are responsible to the strategic decision-makers. We discussed earlier the establishment of functional headquarters. Similarly, United Nations (1993) reports that some transnationals have established '"regional headquarters" ... responsible for coordinating and supporting all activities of all affiliates in a region'. Like functional headquarters, these can be seen as reporting directly to the transnational's top management at its head office, and as freeing the latter to focus on overall coordination of the transnational's activities. Furthermore, the United Nations (1993) analysis is also consistent with the view that the emergence of transnational corporations has contributed to more and more of the world being opened up to more and more manufacturing and indeed other activities. For example, its comments about the European Single Market contributing to transnationals developing integrated production networks to supply Europe as a whole is in line with the view that countries of the Mediterranean Rim have been opened up, a point made earlier in our discussion.

We have been suggesting that under both complex integration strategies (for organizing a firm functionally) and regional strategies (for organizing a firm geographically) strategic decision-making tends to remain centralized at a handful of locations. However, this is not an undisputed view. In particular, recent arguments have suggested that transnationals have been reorganizing themselves along more flexible lines (see Piore and Sabel 1984; Sabel 1988). This reorganization can be seen as part of what the United Nations calls a complex integration strategy. It has been argued that firms are reproducing within themselves the central characteristics which describe sets of autonomous but interrelated firms operating in so-called industrial districts (see the detailed discussion of this argument in Cowling 1991). It has been suggested that they have been inspired to do this in the light of their past failures in adapting to the turbulent conditions of the 1970s and 1980s, of the apparently greater success of the new industrial districts in doing exactly this, and lastly of the challenge offered by the Japanese giants, themselves organized along relatively flexible lines (see Sabel 1988). It has been said that German, Italian and Japanese corporations are moving at the fastest rate with such reorganization, US corporations at the slowest. Under the reorganization it might be argued that, whereas strategic decisions used to be made at the centre and executed within the transnationals' operating units, there is now a reintegration of conception and execution: 'workers and sub-contractors are treated not as programmable automata but as (junior) partners in production with some capacity to reshape the product or production process' (Sabel 1988). The implication would be that our characterization of centralized strategic decision-making by an élite is misplaced, and that we should at least recognize the decentralization of some elements of strategic decision-making to junior partners, but partners nevertheless.

However, we reject this implication. In contrast, our view is that the recent reorganization should be seen as part of a long-term development path along which firms are continuously reorganized to suit strategic decision-makers' objectives but along which strategic decision-making remains the preserve of a centralized core. Any decision to reorganize is made by the centralized core and can be changed by that centralized core. Thus any specific move to mirror characteristics of industrial districts is designed to serve a given set of strategic decision-makers and not to change the composition of that set. Moreover, in saying this we are not denying that some degree of cooperation is always needed in production, and that strategic decision-makers are not all powerful.

Within a firm, strategic decisions are made by an élite. At a point in time these strategic decision-makers are faced by exogenous constraints — as are decision-makers in any situation — and are influenced by others involved with production. These others attempt to influence the decisions that are made but they are distinguished from the decision-makers themselves precisely because they are not making the decisions; they merely apply external pressures on the actual decision-makers. Over time there is variation in the exogenous constraints and external pressures that strategic decision-makers face. With this variation, the actual decisions they make will also vary.

Thus we see a need to be circumspect in interpreting recent moves to reorganize transnational corporations. Flexibility in production is always a concern for strategic decision-makers seeking maximum profits; it is always a consideration when looking to cultivate monopoly power in product markets. However, it becomes a more pressing concern when there is greater uncertainty and turbulence, characteristics firms have typically faced since the 1970s. It is also something that becomes more feasible for strategic decision-makers under certain exogenous constraints and pressures. One of the dangers of greater flexibility for strategic decision-makers is that, other things being equal, it can transfer greater power to workers, subcontractors and lower-level managers. Hence they tend to see greater flexibility as more feasible in periods of, for example, high unemployment because this is a factor undermining worker power. This too has been a characteristic of firms' environment since the 1970s. More generally, a changing emphasis on flexibility related to exogenous economic, social and political events should be expected. We also expect differences across countries depending upon their traditions, institutions and politics, as well as their access to mass markets. For example, it might be speculated that part of the explanation for the greater acceptance of a more cooperative mode of production by German and Japanese firms since 1945 is the effective taming of trade unions in these countries in the early post-war settlement. In the case of the United States the early development of a national mass-market gave a dramatic impetus to perfection of mass-market production modes, within which flexibility was relatively less important. In contrast, the extension of flexible production tends to occur when mass markets diminish, or when a system is threatened by the development of more flexible alternatives.

For Sabel (1988) many giant transnationals are shifting a significant part of decision-making to operating units which are increasingly resembling autonomous firms. Within each operational unit the emphasis is on cooperative teamwork with unions having a 'limited but undeniable responsibility for management'. He suggests that subcontractors are, at one and the same time, more integrated in terms of long-term contracts, design and just-in-time technique, but also less integrated, with the giants encouraging linkages with other customers. Sabel writes of a twofold convergence of large and small firm structures — operating units now have the alertness and flexibility of small firms and they are inserted into a network of small firms, with which they are increasingly similar, with the inter-industry subcontracting network 'cross pollinating techniques'. He supports this description of change with some detailed examples of when it has taken place — Montedison (Italy), Xerox (US), Magna (Canada), Bosch (West Germany) — but he also recognizes that there are many cases where changes are being made but where they are less fundamental. He sees the adoption by many US corporations of Japanese flexible mass production in this light. At the same time he sees Japanese corporations moving on to a more decentralized system with the complete assembly of some products being delegated to leading suppliers and the encouragement of managers and skilled workers to form legally autonomous firms with whom the parent corporation establishes contractual, but not exclusive relationships.

For us there is nothing in these changes to suggest that strategic decision-making has been relocated. Allowing some decision-making to be transferred to operating units does not deny the continuation of a system of central control over the strategy of the organization. Nor does it deny — precisely because of the latter — that the decision to transfer some responsibilities to operating units lies with the centre. What we have seen over recent years is a reorganization of firms in the light of both an ongoing set of concerns, such as flexibility in production, and of changing circumstances, such as greater uncertainty and turbulence. But there has been no fundamental change in the locus of strategic decision-making. Likewise in the future, as conditions change the decision will lie with the centre on whether or not to transfer responsibilities.

Accordingly we suggest that these recent changes do not undermine our characterization of the international economic system. It is a system where strategic decision-makers located in a handful of major cities choose to spread production more or less throughout the world according to the relative attraction of particular locations for achieving strategic decision-makers' objectives. It is a system which simultaneously experiences both centrifugal and centripetal tendencies. The centripetal tendency is associated with strategic decision-making. The centrifugal tendency refers to other production activity moving from core to periphery in the course of economic development as and when barriers to such movement are eroded.

Consequences of transnationals' presence

Our characterization of the nature and essence of the international economic system suggests that various consequences follow from transnational corporations having a significant presence in the world economy. These include the subversion of international trade, centripetalism and short-termism, issues which we will now discuss.

Subverted international trade

One of the features of the international economic system we have depicted is that transnational corporations rely heavily on their ability to trade between their production units in different nations. Indeed, impediments to international trade are one set of barriers to the movement of production activity from core to periphery that we have identified. Hence a crucial feature of an international economic system dominated by transnational corporations is that a high proportion of international trade occurs within transnationals; it is intra-firm trade across national boundaries and thus trade managed in transnationals' interests. This reality is far from the picture imagined in mainstream economic theory, where international trade is characterized as a means by which independent firms obtain access to a market and hence compete with indigenous producers to the benefit of all. As Helleiner and Lavergne (1979) note, in truth,

international trade in manufactured goods looks less and less like the trade of basic economic models in which buyers and sellers interact freely with one another (in reasonably competitive markets) to establish the volume and prices of traded goods. It is increasingly managed by [transnational] corporations as part of their systems of international production and distribution.

The quantitative importance of intra-firm international trade is difficult to specify because of a relative lack of data. Nevertheless, it is an understatement to say that it is significant:

such evidence as does exist is at least suggestive of the very important proportion of world trade which is carried on within the boundaries of [transnationals]. For example, more than fifty per cent of total trade (exports and imports) of both the United States and Japan consists of trade conducted within [transnationals]. Possibly as much as four-fifths of the United Kingdom's manufactured exports are flows of intra-firm trade either within UK enterprises with foreign affiliates or within foreign-controlled enterprises with operations in the United Kingdom. (Dicken 1992)

(See also the relatively more detailed figures reported in Dunning 1993.) For example, the proportion of total UK manufacturing exports and imports accounted for by trade between UK transnationals and their foreign affiliates was 29 per cent and 51 per cent in 1984; comparable figures for Sweden were 29 per cent and 25 per cent in 1975, for Belgium 53 per cent and 48 per cent in 1976, and for Portugal 31 per cent and 34 per cent in 1981.

The importance of international trade to transnationals' activities can also be seen very clearly for firms organizing themselves using the sorts of complex integration strategies and regional strategies that we discussed earlier. The basic idea with both sets of strategies is that a firm carries out different parts of its production activity in different units in dispersed locations, and relies on trade between the units to complete the production of goods and services. For the modern transnational corporation, intra-firm international trade is a tool of production. For example, United Nations (1993) reports on the corporate strategies of automobile producers in manufacturing components and assembling final products. The norm amongst such firms is to produce components in various countries and then to export these to assembly plants. In Western Europe, for example:

after the establishment of the European Community, Ford began to reorganise its production ... A multi-domestic strategy was replaced by a Western Europe-wide strategy. Ford of Europe was established in 1967 as a regional affiliate, and began to integrate the operations of the previously stand-alone national affiliates. Product development, especially between companies in the Federal Republic of Germany and the United Kingdom, was integrated through design and development of the first Europe-wide model, the Capri, in 1969. Falling trade barriers, especially within the European Community, allowed for growing cross-border movements in components and final products. Product development, component manufacturing and final assembly became more integrated throughout Western Europe during the 1970s and 1980s.

Thus within Europe, for instance, 1992 and the Single Market does not mean free trade between independent producers, it means managed trade by transnational corporations. More specifically, free trade allows transnationals' strategic decision-makers to take their firms in directions that are designed to serve the interests of those strategic decision-makers, even though others may prefer something different. An international economic system where trade is free from interference by particular nations is none the less a system of managed trade. The managers are not nations, regions or communities. Rather, they are transnationals' strategic decision-makers. Hence a system of free international trade is in fact one of transnationals' subverted trade.

Centripetalism

Another, and in a sense the most fundamental consequence of the international economic system we have depicted is a centripetal tendency associated with the concentration of strategic decision-making in a handful of the world's major cities. Following Hymer (1972), what this means is that these cities are the centres of dominant economic power. They are the major concentrations of income and wealth, reflecting their status and their authority. They siphon off resources from elsewhere in the international economic system, thereby reducing the capacity of other areas to sustain their own economic development. This in turn retards the political, social and cultural development of these other areas. Centripetal economic tendencies become centripetal political, social and cultural tendencies, the whole system feeding on and reproducing itself.

The key feature of this international system is that economic development in particular nations, regions and communities depends crucially on the position of the nation, region or community in the world order, yet that position is essentially determined by firms' strategic decision-makers. Development depends upon the strategies chosen by an élite.

In the economic system dominated by transnational corporations, it is the transnationals or more specifically their strategic decision-makers who are dictating the rules of the game. Nations, regions and communities are left responding to these rules and are required to fit in with transnationals' wishes if they are to develop. We have suggested that transnationals locate production wherever conditions best serve their objectives. Thus United Nations (1993) cites infrastructural support, low factor costs, technological sophistication and adaptability of the work-force, and open frameworks for trade and investment as particularly important for attracting transnationals' investments. Hence it advocates that nations design industrial economic policies to improve infrastructural support, etc., thereby increasing their attraction to transnationals:

developing countries which do not offer the locational advantages required by regionally or globally integrated firms, such as a skilled labour force, an open trading and investment environment, a developed communication and transport infrastructure and networks of local suppliers on which [transnationals] can draw, risk being further marginalised.

Whilst it might be forcefully argued that dependent development is better than no development, however, we suggest that the real challenge facing nations, regions and communities is to design sets of policies which break them free from dependence on transnationals' strategies. The main thrust of this volume is that overcoming the challenge is not an impossible dream.

Short-termism

Closely related to centripetalism is the idea that particular nations, regions and communities are effectively unable to pursue their long-run future. By its very nature, a particular community may be especially concerned with its long-term position and development; it clearly has a vested interest in seeing that the location it occupies thrives and prospers into the future. However, its basic difficulty is that strategic decision-making in production is based on the wishes of an élite, and generally of an élite in a different locality. Thus crucial decisions about a community's long-term development tend to be made by others who are located elsewhere.

One view is that this may cause problems because at least some of the élite pursue short-term objectives, by choice or otherwise. For example, Cosh *et al.* (1990) discuss evidence concerning takeovers in Britain, Germany and Japan; they conclude that the sort of uninhibited takeover process that has characterized Anglo-Saxon countries may have adversely affected these countries' economic development by shortening firms' time horizons. This conclusion is in line with Charkham's (1989) point that whilst a market for corporate control is highly developed in the United States and Britain, it scarcely exists in Germany and Japan. Moreover, it is consistent with Lewchuck (1986), which explores the decline of British volume car manufacture and picks out the recurring theme of financial institutions demanding short-run returns at the expense of long-run development (see also the more general discussion in Pitt-Watson 1991).

More to the point, however, whether firms plan short-term or long-term they do so in the pursuit of their strategic decision-makers' wishes. This is in no sense long-term planning for the communities in which they do or do not operate. We have suggested that giant transnationals and the international economic system they spawn reserve the vital decision-making function for an élite in a handful of locations; everywhere else in the world is confined to a lower status where fundamental plans are received and implemented, rather than decided upon and evolved. Thus communities do not plan their own long-term futures.

This problem of short-termism and firms' lack of commitment to particular locations *per se* is dramatically illustrated by the deindustrialization argument. We will explore this argument in more detail subsequently in the volume but it is worth mentioning in the current context. Following United Nations (1993), we have suggested that strategic decision-makers will ensure that production activity will be located in whatever country a firm can obtain the highest profits. They have no particular commitment to a specific location and in that respect tend to be fundamentally different from the peoples who live in particular areas. Thus when decisions are being made about a firm's geographical orientation, we expect those decisions to be made in the interests of profit and nothing else. When the conditions for accumulation weaken in any particular country, we are not surprised to see deindustrialization and hence unemployment. The élite strategic decision-makers will ensure that a firm locates production wherever the conditions for accumulation are optimal. Shop-floor workers may object to the implications for their future, as may deserted or ignored communities, but in the current international economic system they are not making the crucial decisions. Again this is well illustrated by events in the British car industry, for example, as discussed in Cowling (1986). It is also illustrated by the case of Ireland in Sweeney (1992b).

Summary

Our aim in this chapter has been to focus directly on the international economic system *per se*, more specifically to discuss the implications for the international economic system of giant transnationals having a significant presence, and thus to consider some further consequences of that presence. Drawing heavily on Hymer (1972), we have suggested that a system dominated by giant transnational corporations is simultaneously subjected to both centrifugal and centripetal tendencies. On the one hand, more and more of the world's economy is being opened up to more and more manufacturing and other activities, but, on the other, strategic decision-making remains concentrated in major cities such as New York, Tokyo, Frankfurt, Paris and London. We have suggested that the joint dominance of these cities will grow with the growth in dominance of the transnationals whose headquarters they contain. This characterization has been explored via a detailed examination of variation in transnationals' structure and organization, looking in particular at corporate strategies over the organization of different functions in a firm, ways that transnationals organize themselves geographically, and arguments about transnationals recently reorganizing themselves along more flexible lines. We have seen nothing in the details of transnationals' structure and organization to undermine our fundamental depiction and much to give it support. It does indeed seem that the current international economic system is one where strategic decision-makers in a handful of major cities choose to spread production more or less throughout the world according to the relative attraction of particular locations for achieving strategic decision-makers' objectives. Whilst strategic decision-making remains concentrated, other production activity moves from core to periphery in the course of economic development as and when barriers to such movement are eroded.

Building on this, we have focused on three systemic features: subverted international trade, centripetalism and short-termism. The very nature of the current international economic system implies these features. We have suggested that intra-firm international trade is a tool of production for the modern transnational, and that so-called free trade is therefore important to their activities. An international economic system where trade is free from interference by particular nations is a system of trade managed by transnationals. We have put considerable emphasis on the centripetal tendency associated with concentrated strategic decision-making and commented on the implications for economic development, income and wealth, as well as for political, social and cultural development. Following on from this, we have highlighted the problem of short-termism; nations, regions and communities are effectively unable to pursue their long-term futures in an international economic system dominated by giant transnationals. Thus we have identified systemic deficiencies which we suggest that communities faced by transnationals need to address; these are issues that should cause fundamental concern because they go to the heart of people's well-being.

4
DIVIDE AND RULE

Previous chapters have identified various systemic features of economies dominated by giant transnational corporations: problems associated with product market monopolization; subversion of international trade; tendencies to centripetalism and short-termism. This chapter focuses on another inherent deficiency of the capitalist economic system: transnationals' use of divide-and-rule strategies towards labour and governments. In doing so it will essentially return to the question of why firms produce in more than one country, an issue addressed in more general terms in Chapter 2. There we argued that the decision to produce in various countries is a strategic choice made by an élite in their interests and despite the wishes of others. Now we will make the more specific argument that an important reason for production in various countries is the use of divide and rule strategies, implying, for example, that profits will be raised at the expense of labour's well-being. We will also return to the discussion in Chapter 3 of the international economic system, including the point that in a system dominated by transnational corporations it is the corporations or more specifically their strategic decision-makers who are dictating the rules of the game; countries' governments are left responding to these rules and are required to fit in with transnationals' wishes if their countries are to develop.

The bulk of the current chapter concentrates on the divide and rule of labour. We will argue that there is an asymmetry of power between labour and the transnational corporation. This asymmetry derives from the corporation's transnationality, which can be exploited by playing on the locational rigidity of labour. We will suggest that by producing in various countries, firms divide their work-force, thereby reducing labour's bargaining power and consequently obtaining lower labour costs. Before this, however, we will consider more briefly the closely related concern that transnationals increase profits by playing off governments in different nations and regions. This is a concern warranting detailed economic and political analysis, which we are in no position to provide at this point; for now, we merely introduce the argument.

The divide and rule of governments

The exact relationship between transnational corporations and governments is a very complex and indeed controversial issue but, whatever the complexities and controversies, it is undoubtedly clear that transnationals routinely bargain with governments for measures enabling the firms to increase their profits. These measures include the introduction and maintenance of favourable investment subsidies, infrastructural support, employment legislation and tax regimes. Moreover, in their bargaining transnationals use the very fact that they can and do produce in various countries. Governments are encouraged to compete against each other under threat of losing a transnational's production or investment; to achieve its own objectives a transnational may switch production and investment, or credibly threaten to do so, wherever conditions in any one nation or region appear relatively disadvantageous.

This divide-and-rule strategy can be seen in practice time and again, although it does not seem to be something that has been systematically evidenced in the literature. For example, Fröbel, Heinrichs and Kreye (1980) discuss the acquisition by Nino AG, a German textile producer, of production facilities in Wexford, Ireland. The views of the chairman of the local development agency[1] are quoted:[2]

you have heard that this German company wishes to extend its operations here in Wexford ... However, the plans for this expansion do not only depend on the state of the economy, but also on how much you people here in Wexford are willing to cooperate with this undertaking ... you should ... bear in mind that we are competing with many other countries in the world to obtain new industries, and that there are development corporations everywhere. We therefore have to convince the investor that he is going to find himself in surroundings which will let him succeed.

This recognizes competition between countries and the willingness by a firm to exploit the competition. At a more general level, Dicken (1992) notes that in recent years 'national governments have struggled to outbid one another in their efforts to secure the large manufacturing plants of the major automobile manufacturers'. He sees this case as an especially good example of a general trend and goes on to observe that 'the giant global corporations of the industry have developed consummate skills in playing one government off against another to secure the maximum advantage from the situation'. See also Bailey, Harte and Sugden (1994) on Britain's policy approach; referring to assistance for inward investors, in 1984 the government argued that 'of course there is a justification for particularly attractive terms to bring to this country internationally mobile projects which otherwise might have arrived in, for example, another part of the European Community and would have free access to our market, but would not provide any jobs'.[3] This competitive approach is also seen in a very recent case involving Britain and France. In 1993 the French government asked the European Commission to investigate aid given by Britain allegedly to entice Hoover to move a vacuum cleaner plant from Dijon to Cambuslang, Scotland. It was reported that a French minister regarded Hoover as using 'Apache tactics', by which he apparently meant that Hoover was scalping different European governments for investment assistance.[4] Concerns were also raised about Britain's opt-out from the European Union's Social Charter, reflecting Britain's general willingness to lower working conditions as a means of attracting investors. At the same time, the French government was worried about alleged Austrian attempts to attract a Grundig plant from Creutzwald (in north-east France) to Vienna.[5]

Hence we suggest that the current economic system is one where transnationals encourage governments to compete with each other in holding down wages, lowering working conditions, and in providing the sort of skilled workers, communication systems and transport infrastructure that transnationals demand. It is a world where transnationals call the tune and governments dance; transnationals dictate strategy and governments respond. This is as much the case when governments compete in holding down wages as when they compete in providing skilled workers; the latter is merely a more progressive form of the low wage approach.

The divide and rule of labour

A firm which seeks profits is clearly concerned with lowering its labour costs. Indeed, we have just been arguing that lower labour costs is an aspect of firms' divide-and-rule strategies with regard to governments. In this section we focus directly on labour costs. More specifically we suggest that a concern with such costs explains why some firms produce in various countries.

One basis for this suggestion might be traditional comparative cost advantage theory. It might be argued that costs of different types of labour vary across countries and that firms will take advantage of this by producing wherever it is cheapest (see, for example, the survey in Koutsoyiannis 1982). But we suggest that this is far too restrictive, because it sees firms as passive reactors to given cost conditions. In fact, costs depend upon the bargaining power of labour and its employers and this is endogenous to firms' decisions, a point dis-cussed fairly extensively in a line of literature looking at the domestic scene (see, for example, Marglin 1974 on the introduction of factories, Richard Edwards 1979 on hierarchy in the work-place, and the reviews of McPherson 1983 and Marginson 1986). Following this line of literature, our view is that an important reason why firms produce in more than one country is divide and rule: by producing in a number of countries firms split up their work-force, with a resultant reduction in labour's bargaining power and labour costs.

We will first of all explore this argument in a theoretical analysis and subsequently look at some empirics. The theory is implicit in such existing works as Fröbel, Heinrichs and Kreye (1980) but we will at least add more detail. As for the empirics, we will attempt to establish divide and rule as a contributory reason for production in various countries. This is obviously limited in so far as it does not attempt to establish the exact influence of divide and rule. Yet it is a valid and useful beginning because many have been very quick to dismiss the explanation on the basis of allegedly widespread evidence that transnationals pay wages at least as high as their rivals.

A theoretical analysis

A firm's labour costs depend upon such factors as wage rates, the effort labour puts into its assigned tasks, the time allowed for tea breaks, and so on. There is a conflict over these costs in that employers and labour will have different optima. This can be seen very clearly in the case of wage rates: for example, with all else being the same — and this includes having a job! — a worker will prefer higher wages than his or her employer. In a perfect labour market this conflict is resolved by competition. For instance, any attempt by a firm to depress wage rates and thereby increase profits would be met by other firms entering the market, paying higher wages and obtaining normal profits. However, this is an unrealistic scenario that can be confined to theoretical day-dreaming. Like the argument in Chapter 2 that firms collude over prices to avoid merely normal profits, should it be necessary they will collude over wages to avoid situations that leave them all worse off (see, for example, the evidence of wage collusion in Forsyth's 1972 survey of Scottish firms). Moreover, when there is an excess supply of labour, collusion will tend to be unnecessary, and as will be seen in the next chapter the world we are depicting has a tendency towards unemployment. In practice, then, the concept of a perfect labour market is a red herring. What actually happens in the real world is that the outcome of their conflict is determined by the bargaining power of labour and employers.

In its turn bargaining power depends very much on the ability of labour to act collectively (see Burkitt and Bowers 1979, for instance).[6] If there is not collective action labour tends to have a weaker bargaining position. This results from various factors, such as:

(a) employers being allowed to replace specific workers by rearranging the activities of others, thereby offsetting any loss of profit resulting from failure to settle the conflict;
(b) increased competition for jobs, greater competition implying a weaker bargaining position;
(c) labour having reduced information on its value to particular employers.

Moreover, the significance of this to us is that collective action is at best very difficult and at worst impossible when people work in different countries.

The reasons for this difficulty are manifest and well documented (see, for example, ILO 1976a and Helfgott 1983). They include such organizational problems as devising institutional arrangements for international trade unions and also more deep-rooted cultural factors such as different languages, xenophobia and different religions. For instance, CIS (1978) talks of the problems faced by Ford workers in

Europe, let alone the world:

it's difficult enough for Ford workers in one country, sharing a common language and separated by comparatively small distances, to organise effectively against the company on anything more than a local plant or shop level. Even here, major problems of communication, sectionalism, and cumbersome national union machinery arise. On a European scale the problems are multiplied many times. Workers in France, Germany, Belgium, Spain and the UK use six different languages plus those of the immigrants. It means much greater distances — over a thousand miles from Halewood to Valencia, with disproportionately large travel and tele-phone costs as a result. There are that many more unions — and another layer, the international union organisation, on top.

In principle it should be possible to overcome the purely organiza-tional problems without too much difficulty. After all, transnational corporations provide an indication of how activities can be organized where large distances are involved. But fundamental problems are posed by the cultural factors for which there is no easy solution. Indeed, they reveal a basic asymmetry between labour and its employers at the international level. Labour tends to be locationally rigid, often having close human and physical ties to a particular region and being very strongly influenced by a particular region's his-tory and culture (see again the discussion of short-termism in the pre-vious chapter). This can raise major barriers to collective action, because such action requires a considerable amount of cooperation. In contrast, employers have by no means as many problems in operating successfully across national borders. First, wherever a firm operates employers talk a common language and have a common religion: profit. Second, simply pursuing profits across the world does not require the same level of cooperation by people from different coun-tries that would be demanded of labour for it to act collectively. Rather, pursuing profits essentially requires an appropriate hierar-chical organization into which people can be slotted. This is more a problem of coordination than of cooperation.

All of this clearly suggests that a firm may produce in various coun-tries so that it can face a more fragmented work-force, with the conse-quent advantages of reducing labour's bargaining power and labour costs.[7]

To illustrate, suppose a firm manufactures shirts in two stages: cut-ting and then the sewing of cloth. Assume that initially all of its man-ufacturing facilities are in Britain and that its work-force is united, quick to seize the opportunity to act collectively to maintain working conditions. For example, if the firm tries to reduce the quality of working life for the cutters the entire work-force is prepared to strike, completely halting production. The firm can respond to this in various ways. One possibility is to transfer part of both its cutting and sewing operations to, say, the Philippines. Then, even if its work-force in Britain has a grievance which leads it to strike, while work continues in the Philippines the firm can indefinitely maintain at least partial supply to its customers.[8] A second option is to divide its work-force by transferring the sewing operation to the Philippines. A case when this might be preferable is if the firm doubts the skill of Philippino workers to do the cutting. The transfer will still reduce labour's bargaining power in certain circumstances. For instance, if the firm now tries to reduce the quality of working life for cutters, production will not stop as long as there are stocks of cut cloth to supply sewers in the Philippines and those sewers are willing to work.[9]

This is not to deny that even without transferring any production outside Britain the firm could undermine strikes. For example, it could build up stocks of finished goods to enable supplies to customers to continue at least for a while. But the critical point is that the possibilities for reducing labour's bargaining power by producing in various countries give added degrees of freedom — more room to manœuvre. Nor are the possibilities of transferring operations to the Philippines the firm's only options. It has many others. It could transfer activity to somewhere other than the Philippines, or divide its work-force amongst three, four, five or even more countries.

The choice it makes will depend upon many factors, such as the skill of workers in one part of the world versus those elsewhere, and its expectations of labour 'militancy' in Europe as compared to Asia. Also important will be the attitudes of governments in different locations and the extent to which these can be influenced by the firm. This brings us back to the earlier discussion. Governments can directly influence labour costs — for example, by such obvious means as legislation affecting working hours or the right to strike, but also by more subtle ways such as encouraging greater effort from labour. Moreover, the attitudes of governments are not independent of firms' wishes, rather they are endogenous to firms' activities. Both of these points can be seen in the earlier discussion of Nino AG's acquisition of production facilities in Ireland and the other examples concerning divide and rule by governments.

Another important factor will be the types of organizational form at the firm's disposal. The significance of organizational form to firms producing in more than one country was recognized in general by Hymer (1972). Using the United States as an illustration, he noted the growth of Marshallian firms into large corporations requiring completely different forms of organization, especially the so-called multidivisional form. He argued that this helped to provide the 'power to go abroad' because it gave firms an appropriate administrative structure. However, with the more specific issue of divide and rule leading to production in various countries, we suggest that the choice between market and non-market activity is especially interesting.

We have argued (in Chapter 2) that a firm is the means of coordinating production from one centre of strategic decision-making and that this coordination can include both market and non-market activity. Thus suppose the shirt manufacturer in our example decides to respond to a militant work-force by dividing its sewing operations between the Philippines and Britain. One possibility is to set up factories in both countries and have nothing to do with the market until the final goods are sold to the consumers. Another may be to subcontract the sewing to small workshops dotted throughout Britain and the Philippines. This would involve market exchanges because the workshops would be contracted to do sewing in consideration for a specified sum of money. But provided production was being coordinated from one centre of strategic decision-making, there would still be only one firm. Moreover the subcontracting option may be particularly appealing to a firm because it can provide an extreme division of a militant work-force. For instance, whilst those Ford workers employed in huge plants clearly identified with the Ford Motor Company find organizing collective action very difficult, imagine the problems of workers dotted across the world in small workshops operating under completely different names. How many would even begin to recognize that they work for the same firm? Simply attempting to organize collective action would be a nightmare. Actually doing so might be impossible.

Having said this, a firm will not necessarily use the subcontracting option. It may be impossible because of limitations in available technology; some production activity cannot be carried out in small workshops. Perhaps there is neither a system of small workshops readily available nor the possibility of establishing such a system in an appropriate time period. Furthermore it may be simply unnecessary, for example, because a work-force can be broken into a very weak body with no real bargaining power without resort to such extreme division. It may be sufficient to locate one plant in the Philippines, another in Britain and rely on (or perhaps promote) racial tension to keep labour in the two completely alienated.

In a moment we will consider empirical evidence concerning the divide-and-rule hypothesis but, before turning to this, it is worth emphasizing two points about our theoretical argument. First, as an explanation for why firms produce in various countries its focus is distribution and not Pareto efficiency; distribution is the very essence of the bargaining analysis. This compares starkly with mainstream economic approaches to why firms produce in various countries (see again Chapter 2). The thrust of our argument is that a firm may produce in different countries to weaken the bargaining power of its work-force and thereby to increase profits at the expense of that work-force. Of course, labour is likely to realize this. Attempts will therefore be made to prevent a firm producing in various countries by agreeing to lower labour costs if it will produce in just one country. This may appeal to a firm if it can thereby avoid any extra costs that may result from producing in various countries — for example what the Hymer (1960)/Kindleberger (1969) approach calls 'costs of operating at a distance'. However, production in various countries will still be the outcome in some situations if for no other reason than the fact that bargaining is by its very nature a game of bluff and counter-bluff. For instance a work-force may not believe an employer's demand for lower wages to prevent the transfer of production, yet if the employer's bluff is called and the work-force is shown to be wrong, production will be transferred.

A second point worth emphasizing concerns the international division of labour. The divide-and-rule analysis implies the spreading of production activity throughout the world. The exact locations firms use will depend upon the sorts of factors we have mentioned, but firms will establish production sites in many places. For example, unskilled activity knows few geographical bounds. Moreover production technology is endogenous to the wishes of strategic decision-makers, who will therefore seek the technology they find most desirable (see Marglin 1974). Over time, for example, firms will develop technology which deskills more and more activity, thereby opening more and more of the world to their production activity. We suggest that the benefits to strategic decision-makers of dividing and ruling labour are an incentive for such changes. The implication is that the desire to divide and rule undermines the 'old' international division of labour. The old division saw the countries of the world split into industrial and primary producers, international trade being carried out between the two. The industrial countries bought raw materials and agricultural products from the primary producers, who in return imported manufactured goods. However, the 'new' division cuts through this simple dichotomy (see also the evidence and discussion in Hymer 1972, Adam 1975, and Fröbel, Heinrichs and Kreye 1980). This is an argument which dovetails with our discussion of the international economic system in Chapter 3; there we characterized the nature and essence of the system and here we are exploring a determinant of the system's detailed structure.

Some empirical evidence

A usual reaction to the divide-and-rule hypothesis is to reject it on the basis of evidence on wage levels in different types of firm. The argument is that transnationals appear to pay wages at least as high as their rivals and that therefore production in various countries cannot be founded on a division of the work-force to lower labour costs. The apparent evidence for this comes from many studies covering many countries (see, for example, ILO 1976b and the very recent survey in Dunning 1993). Typical is the analysis in Buckley and Enderwick (1983) and Blanchflower (1984). This examines senior managements' estimates of employees' average weekly gross pay in British manufacturing plants using data from the 1980 *Workplace Industrial Relations Survey*. The conclusion is that, in general, non-UK-owned plants offer comparable or higher wages than UK-owned plants. However, we suggest that in fact this is consistent with divide and rule.

First, no distinction is drawn between transnationals and their rivals. Correspondingly there is no relevant evidence of relative wages. The difficulty here is in part one of definition; reference to plant ownership does not and cannot capture the full extent of a transnational's activities. Rather, control is the key concept. What is likely to be especially important is that the data ignore subcontracting arrangements, which we have already argued are significant to the divide-and-rule approach. Moreover the difficulty is also because a UK-owned plant could be as much a part of a transnational as a non-UK-owned plant; the distinction therefore fails to pick out transnationals. Thus if UK-owned transnationals are particularly successful at dividing their work-force across the world, they can pay sufficiently low wages to allow non-UK-owned plants to pay more than UK-owned plants, whilst transnationals pay less than their rivals.

Secondly, even where transnationals do pay more they may nevertheless be founded upon the divide-and-rule concept. Keeping the focus on wages, this is best seen by an illustration. Suppose firm i is a wage leader in country X and that it acquires production facilities in country Y. It is perfectly feasible for i to be a high payer in Y — for example, because it feels high wages will attract better workers — yet still pay less than if it produced solely in X facing a work-force acting collectively. For instance, it could still undermine bargaining power in X by diverting production from Y to bypass a strike. Moreover this is all consistent with its remaining a wage-leader in country X — for instance, because it continues to face the best-organized work-force in X, albeit a work-force which now has less bargaining power than before. In short, then, a firm can produce in two countries and be a high payer in both, even though the basis of its transnational production is divide and rule.

Furthermore, even more important is the fact that wages must only be a part of the story. This is fatal to any claim that wages evidence refutes the divide-and-rule hypothesis; quite simply, the hypothesis centres on labour *costs* and therefore includes many other factors. Forget the wages transnationals pay — what about the effort put into jobs, the time allowed for lunches and the conditions in which work is carried out? Even if transnationals do pay higher wages than their rivals it is undoubtedly clear that their labour costs may nevertheless be lower.[10]

To argue successfully that divide and rule is an important reason for firms to produce in more than one country, however, we must be more positive. It is not enough simply to refute the wages view because this only removes an obstacle from our path. What is needed is evidence that goes to the heart of the hypothesis, something which wages analysis is incapable of doing. Unfortunately this is not easy to come by, because divide and rule is not an issue that has occupied researchers' attention to any substantial degree. Nevertheless, some evidence is available (see Cowling and Sugden 1987).

One source is the view of participants in firms. Strongly suggestive are the views of the trade unionists summarized by ILO (1976a). It refers to 'union concerns' that transnationals 'deliberately' dual-source at least some of their activities — i.e. they establish alternative sources of supply — so that they can 'thereby reduce the impact of a strike in any one country'. More generally it also comments that:

one of the most serious charges which unions make, from time to time, *vis-à-vis* [transnationals] is that the latter *use their internally-spread facilities as a threat to counter union demands and power*. If the union will not yield the company can or will threaten to transfer its production to another country, or the company may utilise already existing facilities in another country to penalise the 'demanding' union, or the company may threaten to curtail its future investments in the country in which the union is making 'unreasonable' (in the company's judgment) demands. All of these tactics are subsumed by the unions under the general head of threats to shift production as part of the labour tactics of multinational enterprises. (emphasis added)[11]

This is supported by 'typical' views from various European unions. For example, the British Trades Union Congress feels that 'in many companies the existence of alternative sources of supply gives management scope to threaten to switch products to other locations. *This can be a very effective bargaining counter*' (emphasis added).[12] Similarly, the Swedish Metalworkers' Union suggests that '[transnational] companies have wide opportunities of moving their capital from one country to another. *This ... makes it more difficult for trade union organisations to pursue their demands* for higher wages, employment and workers' influence in the firm' (emphasis added).[13] In so far as these views are representative they certainly imply that firms do use the divide-and-rule strategy.

This conclusion is also supported by Greer and Shearer's (1981) survey of US unions.[14] A third of the (six) unions reporting on the issues claim that firms actually use foreign production to undercut the bargaining position of US unions and actually undermine US strikes using foreign production. Particularly interesting and clear-cut is the claim from two (out of seven) unions that firms strengthen their US bargaining position by moving their production or making new investments abroad.

It is possible that this is all in the imagination of trade unionists but that is unlikely. Moreover, even firms are willing to admit their use of divide-and-rule tactics. There is no widespread evidence of this but the remarkable thing is that it does exist. Transnationals seem to be very sensitive to adverse publicity and accordingly the use of divide-and-rule strategies is hardly something they will wish to advertise (see ILO 1976a). Yet Greer and Shearer (1981) report a survey of companies in the United States, each of which is non-US-owned.[15] Seven out of twenty-six firms reporting on the issue agreed that they would consider using production in various countries to discourage US strikes. One out of twenty-eight said that it had actually done so. This is also supported by ILO's (1976a) reference to the Chrysler Corporation chairman extolling the benefits of dual-sourcing *vis-à-vis* bargaining power. In other words, then, even firms agree that trade unionists are not paranoid in their view of firms' activities — at least, not paranoid all of the time.

The implication from all of this is that divide and rule does indeed lead to the presence of transnationals. The evidence certainly goes to the heart of the matter because it literally asks participants on either side of the labour cost conflict what they think is happening. Trade unionists seem in little doubt. But they are even joined by some firms.

For those who remain sceptical there is also the evidence of specific situations. This is sparse and again there is the problem of firms not wishing to advertise their activities. Nevertheless, instances are discussed in the literature at odd times. For example, ILO (1976a) mentions the case of labour unrest in Britain leading the Chrysler Corporation to contemplate the transfer of production to sister operations in France and/or Japan, and Gennard (1972) refers to the antics of the Goodyear Tyre Company in using supplies from elsewhere to undermine industrial action in Britain. See also Harte and Sugden (1990) on the dealings of General Motors with Vauxhall workers over the siting of a new engine plant, and the claims in early 1993 that Hoover played off workers in France and Scotland.[16] Moreover, the activities of Ford in Europe have been comparatively well documented.

The clearest possible case of divide and rule is provided by the CIS (1978) report of Ford's decision deliberately to dual-source components for its Fiesta model to reduce labour's bargaining power. This is shown by its engines policy:

in the event of a shutdown of the Dagenham Fiesta engine line, the company's aim would be to boost output of the Valencia engine line to supply extra units to the Dagenham and Saarlouis assembly lines. With a higher output of the Valencia engined cars from these two plants, stocks of the Dagenham engines could be stretched out to minimise interruptions in supply of any model. Similarly if the Valencia engine plant were shut down.

This also shows how Ford uses more than one assembly point, a fact picked out by Friedman (1977) in his discussion of multi-sourcing in the car industry. See also United Nations (1993), which identifies a reason for Ford establishing both multiple component plants and multiple assembly plants during the 1970s and 1980s as the means by which to offset work stoppages throughout Western Europe.

More subtle is the continuous barrage of threats Ford has hurled at its work-force down the years. One of the bargaining strategies commonly used by all firms is to argue that unless labour costs are lowered immediately the prospects for future investment are bleak. A firm certainly need not be a transnational to do this. But when it is, it has the added ability convincingly to threaten workers in any one country that failure to accept lower labour costs now will mean future investment elsewhere in the transnational's global empire. This can be credible precisely because it does have a global empire. This is in contrast to a firm producing in one country and facing a united work-force; there is then no 'elsewhere' to throw in their faces (at least not in such a credible sense).

Ford's use of this strategy is clearly felt by Friedman (1977) to be an important feature of its industrial relations.[17] More specifically this is shown in Steuer and Gennard's (1971) report that in February 1970 Henry Ford was questioned by Halewood shop stewards. They were concerned about rumours of new investment going to Germany rather than Britain, it being known that Detroit was unhappy with British industrial relations. This story is taken up by ILO (1976a). In 1971 there was a strike at Ford in Britain.

While this dispute was underway ... Henry Ford ... was reported to have declared that parts of the Ford Escort and Cortina models ... would in future no longer be made in the United Kingdom but would be manufac-tured in Asia ... Mr Ford came to London shortly thereafter, and in a meeting with (then) British Prime Minister Heath, he is reported to have let it be known, with regard to the company's labour difficulties, that if improvements were not forthcoming, the company would take its busi-ness elsewhere.

Furthermore, the threats are seemingly not empty:

in 1973 when the company decided to locate the bulk of its small car engine production in the United States (for the Pinto model, sold largely in the United States), the *Financial Times* (22 June) reported: 'It is no secret that industrial disputes in Britain priced the United Kingdom out of the market ...'. The same paper added, 'There was, of course, no guarantee that Britain would ever have been selected for such a major development but the comments of Henry Ford ... (in) the early part of the year made it clear that the United Kingdom had dropped out of the running ...'. The same report added, 'the fear of similar labour unrest in Germany in the future may have entered into the company's decision to locate the plant in the United States.

Meanwhile, coming more up to date, it is clear from *Financial Times* reports that the threats at Ford were continuing. Ford's employee relations director, Paul Roots, is said to have told British unions in 1983 that labour costs were too high: '"this year, to date, we have achieved only 62 to 64 per cent of capacity at Halewood and

Dagenham against 100 per cent at Saarlouis in West Germany and 96 percent at Valencia, Spain," he said. "If we do not get our costs down we cannot compete and if we cannot compete we will not survive in Britain as a manufacturing company"'.[18] The following year Ford of Europe's then vice president for manufacturing, Mr Hayden, delivered the same message to those in dispute with the company over investment plans: 'although Mr Hayden denied that Ford was running down its British plants, he gave a stiff warning that the consequences for future investment would be serious if the productivity gap with European plants was not closed'.[19] And coming into the 1990s, the saga continues. For example, in February 1992 the workforce at the Dagenham and Halewood assembly plants was warned in no uncertain terms that it should catch up with performance at Ford's equivalent operations elsewhere in Europe. The chairman of Ford of Europe argued: 'it isn't the facilities that are different [to those in continental Europe], there is not a damn thing wrong with the Halewood facility. It is the way labour is organised and the way labour functions ... You have to close the gap [with continental Europe] eventually or you will have to shift capacity — because otherwise you will have to say to hell with it'.[20] This followed a warning to Dagenham workers earlier in 1992 that improved productivity in Fiesta production was needed if they were to be sure of their role in producing the model's successor.[21] Clearly little has changed down the years.

This leaves us with a catalogue of instances that can permit little doubt that divide and rule is important to understanding the activities of one of the largest companies in the world. The difficulty with this sort of evidence is that it is uncertain just how typical Ford is, but it seems extremely unlikely that it is very unusual. Rather, we can reasonably expect Ford to be typical. So this is also clear evidence that divide and rule of labour is an important reason for production in more than one country. Again it goes to the heart of the matter and again it points to a clear conclusion. If Ford sees divide and rule as an opportunity for increased profits, so also will others. Indeed, the very fact that Ford can be seen to use the strategy means that others will do likewise on the basis that if it can yield profits for Ford it can yield profits for them. What is good enough for Ford will be good enough for other firms.

This does not imply that a good strategy for Ford necessarily means good all round. It would indeed suggest increased profits, but at the same time it could create worsening working conditions and lower wages. For somebody, somewhere might be made to pay for the rise in profits.

Notes

1 This is not strictly speaking a government. However, throughout this discussion the term government includes a nation's or region's public agencies in general.
2 From the economic supplement of the German newspaper, *Frankfurter Allgemeine Zeitung*.
3 Norman Tebbitt, then Trade and Industry Secretary, quoted from *The Financial Times*.
4 *Financial Times*, 29 January 1993.
5 ibid.
6 It is not simply collective bargaining that is at issue. For instance, contacts by workers to foster information-sharing are important (see, for example, Enderwick 1985).
7 This hypothesis sees a firm dividing its work-force when it actually produces in various countries. A counterpart is where firms contemplating new investment divide potential employees.
8 In his 'eclectic theory' Dunning (1980) suggests that transnationals may be able to 'reduce the impact of strikes or industrial unrest in one country by operating parallel production capacity in another'.
9 The comparison being made here is a firm manufacturing shirts by cutting and sewing cloth in Britain versus a firm doing the same thing but in Britain and the Philippines. This is not to deny that different comparisons could be made — for example, between the bargaining power of labour when it is employed by a firm whose sole activity is to cut cloth in Britain and when it is employed by a firm which cuts cloth in Britain and sews this into shirts in the Philippines. Then labour in Britain may have more bargaining power when it is part of the wider operation encompassing the Philippines, other things being equal (for example, because a strike in Britain would cause disruption in the Philippines by stopping work there once any stock of cut cloth were exhausted). But introducing these other comparisons does not undermine our divide-and-rule analysis; its very point is to take the activities of a particular firm and compare labour costs when *those* activities are carried out in one versus more than one country.
10 Steuer and Gennard (1971), referring to Britain, note: 'the foreign subsidiary, particularly the American-owned firm, is alleged to utilise labour more effectively, which could be a nice way of saying people work harder'. Nevertheless, it is also worth pointing out that our earlier analysis explaining why wage rates could be higher in transnationals might also explain why labour costs could be higher. Thus it might explain, for instance, what ILO (1976b) refers to as the widely accepted proposition that in underdeveloped countries conditions of work are often superior in transnationals.
11 Strictly speaking, the use of internationally spread facilities to counter union power does not mean that this is why the facilities were spread

in the first place. But it is certainly a strong indication.

12 Comments from a conference report.

13 Statement from a congress.

14 They surveyed fifty unions in all, thirteen having experience with non-US-owned companies.

15 They surveyed twenty-nine companies in all.

16 *Financial Times*, 5 March 1993.

17 'One of the most significant features of industrial relations in the UK motor industry from the mid-1960s has been the ever-present threat, particularly coming from Chrysler and Ford, to shift operations to other countries' (Friedman, 1977).

18 29 October 1983. Friedman (1977) refers to Ford using the pace of production in its continental plants as 'a yardstick and a driving stick' for its work-force in Britain.

19 23 February 1984.

20 17 February 1992.

21 14 January 1992.

5
A FUTURE OF STAGNATION?

In the introductory chapter to the book we described the performance of economies occupying different positions in the world economic system: the high and persistent levels of unemployment in many of the advanced industrial countries, and their often rather poor levels of productivity growth; the present low level of development within the developing countries despite the considerable achievements of the earlier post-Second World War period; the dramatic crisis within Central and Eastern Europe and the former Soviet Union as they attempt the transition from state socialism to free market economies. It is undoubtedly a picture of unrelieved gloom, with the significant exceptions of Japan (qualified by the present politico-economic turmoil) and other East Asian economies, such as South Korea, Taiwan and Singapore, but also China and Vietnam, who are taking a rather different route into the market economy. Subsequent chapters have begun to piece together an explanation of this generally poor economic performance by seeking to understand the nature, behaviour and impact of the major actors within free market economies, the giant, transnational corporations. We have focused on the growth in power of the transnationals and its implications for the workings of both the market for goods and the market for labour. In that context we uncovered a range of systemic deficiencies within the free market system which arise from the concentration of strategic decision-making. In this chapter we shall address the question as to whether or not this evolution of a dominant transnationalism within the free market economy can explain its current tendency to stagnate.

It has frequently been argued that the development of the monopoly capitalist system will, sooner or later, lead to a stagnationist tendency rather than some long-run, full employment equilibrium.

We will present the basic monopoly capitalism argument before going on to examine more directly the implications of the transnational control of production and markets by the dominant firms in the system for this evolutionary process, and in so doing we shall unearth supply-side arguments in addition to the essentially demand-side arguments we analyse earlier. Is the issue of stagnation likely to be more or less pressing in a world dominated by such transnational organizations? Our analysis points fairly unambiguously towards the conclusion that stagnation is a more pressing issue in such a world, not only because it becomes more likely, but also because it becomes more unmanageable without radical changes in the way the international economy is organized. Thus we would predict a future of stagnation for a world organized as it is today, but a future we can avoid if we learn and act as democratic communities.

The basic monopoly capitalism argument[1]

The argument advanced in the monopoly capitalism literature is that monopolizing tendencies within the older industrialized countries of the world would lead to a stagnationist tendency due to a deficiency of aggregate demand within that part of the world economic system and this in turn would lead to a more general stagnation.[2] We start the analysis with the prediction and observation of substantial increases in concentration in most markets, enhanced and sustained by rising transnationalism. This in turn is expected to lead to an increase in prices relative to marginal costs (see Chapter 3) and therefore to an increase in the share of profits plus overheads in value-added.[3] The potential therefore exists for an increase in the share of profits in aggregate income, but whether this is realized depends on the impact of the monopolization process on aggregate demand. The immediate impact of rising monopolization would be a downward revision in planned investment in line with the planned reduction in the rate of output within those sectors where the degree of monopoly has increased — the higher price is associated with a lower level of sales. The reduction in aggregate investment, in the absence of compensating adjustments elsewhere, would lead to a reduction in the level of profits in the whole system, which would lead in turn to further cutbacks in investment and thus generate a cumulative process of decline. Compensating, upward adjustments in investment elsewhere may, of course, take place, for example, via a process of diversification, with expected funds from the monopolizing process at the level of the individual firm being allocated to new lines of production, but such adjustments are likely to involve considerable lags and in the meantime the cumulative process of decline will already have set in. As Steindl (1952) concluded in his path-breaking study of the twentieth-century evolution of the US economy, 'development of monopoly ... is ... the main explanation of the decline in the rate of growth of capital which has been going on in the US from the end of the last century. This is not to say that other factors have not played a role ...' He also argued that a continuing decline in the rate of growth was possible.

But, if not investment, can increased consumption be expected to take up the slack and help to maintain the level of aggregate demand so that monopoly profits can be realized? This is unlikely to happen fast enough, nor to the required extent, given that profit recipients receive their income less frequently than wage earners and also tend to have much lower propensities to consume (see, for example, Pitelis 1982). There is also the question as to whether such households will expect to have access to the increased flow of profits. For a variety of reasons corporations prefer to retain profits rather than distribute them. But what about rising managerialism, reflected in rising intra-corporate consumption out of non-reported profits — that is, all those expenditures within the corporation which contribute directly to managerial utility, but which represent a deduction from profits? We are thinking here of many, perhaps most of the trappings of office — could these expenditures provide at least a partial antidote to any demand deficiency? The importance of such expenditures (see Williamson 1964) is such as to warrant serious attention; the managerial hierarchy in the major corporations shows a remarkable capacity for absorbing increases in income flows into the corporation. However, although in aggregate, by tending to maintain demand, managerialism serves to maintain profits, it will be seen as something to be minimized by those interested in the flow of reported profits. Thus although the growth of giant firms operating in oligopolistic markets gives rise to a substantial growth in managerial discretion arising as a result of their increasing isolation from the sanctions of both capital and product markets, with all the associated expenditures that is likely to entail, such discretion will inevitably lead to measures to curtail it, at least at all levels of the hierarchy below the actual top level! The innovation of efficient internal control systems, like the multi-divisional organizational form which decentralizes operational responsibility to production divisions whilst centralising control of capital flows, thus creating an efficient and well-informed internal capital market (see Williamson 1970), will impose very real limits on the ability of managerial capitalism to overcome a latent tendency to stagnation.

Other adjustments are possible. Aggregate demand could be maintained via a growing net export surplus, but there is little reason to suppose that this is likely to follow a rise in the degree of monopoly within a particular economy; indeed, just the reverse could happen (for an inter-industry analysis of the United States, see Koo and Martin 1984). Consider also the current balance of payments positions of the United States and Japan. The United States has demonstrated a strong, *concentrating* tendency over the 1980s (Attaran and Saghafi 1988), coupled with the growth of a substantial trade *deficit*, whereas Japan has experienced (in some ways) a *deconcentrating* trend (Adams and Brock 1988), coupled with an increasing trade *surplus*. If the rise in the degree of monopoly is a general trend within the world industrial system as a whole, as indeed appears to be the case (with the significant exception of Japan) (see Amin and Dietrich 1991 for the case of the European Union), then it is even less likely that a growing export surplus could be maintained over an extended period, since it would raise the issue of how the rest of the world's growing trade deficit was to be financed. The present international debt crisis could be seen as a consequence of a rising degree of monopoly in the industrial and energy sectors of the world economy. This led to the recent calamitous fall in the commodity terms of trade (commodity price index ÷ manufactures price index) reported by Maizels (1992) (see chapter 1), and the imposed, deflationary response, orchestrated by the IMF/World Bank, has further deepened the world slump.

Aggregate demand could also be maintained by reducing the propensity to save via advertising and product innovation (see Keir 1993 for a survey and some recent estimates), and we can rely on the system of monopoly capitalism to generate just such a response, given that oligopolistic rivalry often takes on these dimensions. But this sort of investment would seem incapable of properly fulfilling this role given its essentially procyclical character (again see Keir 1993). Whilst we are concerned with a long-term tendency, this is not separable from the process of cyclical fluctuation. Advertising and product innovation tend to mimic the behaviour of investment in general and therefore seem ill equipped to fill the role of replacing investment within the structure of aggregate demand. The time when a thrust to consumption provided by advertising and product innovation is needed is just the time when these sort of expenditures are being reined back.

Thus we are suggesting that the internal forces of the capitalist free market system cannot be relied on to maintain a level of aggregate demand sufficient to sustain full employment within a general monopolizing trend. But salvation may be sought outside the system, or at least within the political sphere rather than the economic sphere of the capitalist system. If all else fails, governments can step in to manage aggregate demand in order to secure the full employment of resources. Without intruding into the inner workings of the capitalist economy, government would simply set a different, and higher level of demand to which the free market would respond. Thus the negative impact of a rising degree of monopoly on aggregate demand could be fully offset by a rising budget deficit. But we cannot necessarily assume this response, although at first sight it may appear beneficial from all points of view. We have seen, during our recent history, how monetarism replaced Keynesianism, not only within Thatcher's Britain but also earlier within Callaghan's Britain and more generally within the national governments and supra-national institutions of the world's advanced industrial countries and beyond. As long ago as 1979, the IMF, the World Bank, the OECD and the GATT were as one in demanding a move back from Keynesian policies — for them demand management was dead. The apparently Keynesian policies of the Reagan administration in the United States arose largely fortuitously out of the supply-side economics (e.g. tax-cutting) and military expansion of that period. What was most remarkable about the US case was that despite the continuing substantial budget deficit the economy shows no sustained propensity to generate full employment. It remains to be seen how Clintonomics actually turns out, but meanwhile the European Union is still espousing a monetarist course on Economic and Monetary Union, despite problems with ERM, and the transition in Central and Eastern Europe and the former Soviet Union is still driven by monetarist principles. It is clear that governments generally in the late twentieth century have no obvious nor strong commitment to full employment, a topic we shall enquire into later.

It may be concluded that although mechanisms are available to mitigate any stagnationist tendency precipitated by a tendency for the degree of monopoly to increase, none is automatic. It would therefore appear that a stagnationist tendency could be seen as an inevitable consequence of the maturing of the monopoly capitalist system: not an inevitable outcome at any particular period of history — major political or economic events can put these underlying forces into abeyance for long periods, as the Second World War and its enormous consequences did for the middle third of the twentieth century — but nevertheless an inevitable consequence at some stage in the unravelling of the monopoly capitalist system. Some, nevertheless, will argue that a slump in demand will induce a price-cutting response and thus remove the initial cause of the slump. Indeed, it may be conjectured that the impact of a substantial fall in demand may cause an oligopoly group, which has settled on a particular *modus vivendi*, to fly apart. Each member of the group observes that its own sales have dropped and assumes the worst on the part of its rivals: that they have been engaged in aggressive price-cutting, or similar market-share-augmenting activities. Each member of the group therefore responds with similar strategies, tit-for-tat. However, given that the explanation for the original observation of a fall in sales was in fact a general slump in demand, this will gradually become more obvious to the group, more quickly in the case of the transnationals with their superior detection power, as argued in Chapter 2. Faced with such mutual adversity we may anticipate that the group will tend to come together to solve its mutual problems, to establish a new *modus vivendi* under the new circumstances. Thus the initial impact of the downturn in demand may well be a reduction in price-cost margins, but if the slump persists we can expect to see a recovery in margins as the degree of cohesion within the oligopoly group increases in the face of common adversity. Evidence is available to support this conjecture in the case of the United Kingdom (Cowling 1983; Conyon 1992), and the United States (Bils 1987). Thus it would seem that stagnationist tendencies will not be fully alleviated by a reversion to more competitive behaviour with the onset of a slump. It is of the nature of oligopolistic interaction that firms operating within such groups, and they tend now to be ubiquitous, will assume a behaviour that prolongs slumps originally precipitated by their collective action. This can appear entirely rational within their own micro-context, but adds up to aggregate behaviour against their joint interests.

Transnationalism and demand-side explanations

We have presented the outlines of the monopoly capitalism explanation of stagnation, but we have done this in a way that concentrates on the evolution of stagnationist forces within a specific national economy. The present system of monopoly capitalism as we approach the twenty-first century has become increasingly dominated by giant economic organizations with a transnational base, as we reported in Chapter 2. This domination of the free market economy by organizations with an international ambit requires a reassessment of the original monopoly capitalist explanation of stagnation. We shall argue that in this new world of the transnationals the stagnation of demand has become a more pressing issue, not only because it has become more likely, but also because it has become more unmanageable.

First, as extensively explored in Chapter 2, transnationalism is one of the mechanisms whereby the monopolization tendency evolved, just as the nationalization tendency of capital led to the growth of monopoly or oligopoly at the national level, as national corporations were founded. Moreover, transnationalism has introduced an additional element of control over the market — it brings control by giant firms to the pattern and dimensions of trade (see Chapter 3). Thus transnationalism undermines the possible impact of trade in restraining monopoly or oligopoly pricing behaviour within national markets as well as promoting collusion within such markets via the development of multi-market contacts, etc. In the process of establishing such control these giant firms may engage in various forms of economic warfare, the outcome of which in the transitional period may be a reduction in price, although even this outcome is less likely than advertising and product rivalry, which will tend to enhance rather than undermine the degree of monopoly by a process of differentiation. Recent evidence suggests that within the European car markets, exchange rate fluctuations have not been seen as opportunities to engage in price competition (see Cowling and Sugden 1989).

Second, transnationalism results in a greater imbalance of power between capital and labour since it facilitates a process of divide and rule and therefore tends to hold down wage costs which may have implications for the share of wages in national income and hence for aggregate demand, given the higher propensity to consume of wage earners as compared with profit recipients (see Chapter 4). Similarly it serves, by the same process, to contain the salary rates of the lower levels of the managerial hierarchy — the positions of higher levels, the strategic staff at the core of these giant firms, will not be eroded by transnationalism; indeed, the empires they control will be constantly augmented by the evolution of transnationalism, and thus their status in the economy and in society at large. Such developments will tend to reinforce the direct effects of monopolization on distribution.

Third, the existence of a transnational production base itself contributes to the tendency for prices to be held in periods of recession. A recession in one country can lead to plant closure in that country, with the market being sourced from foreign plants. Without control of foreign production facilities firms may be forced to operate domestic plants at inefficient rates of output, were the degree of monopoly to be maintained — there would be a lesser incentive to preserve or enhance the degree of cohesion or collusion within the oligopoly group. Thus the growth of transnational firms allows for the more flexible adjustment of production to falling demand and thereby serves to hold price levels (or raise them) when otherwise they may have fallen, as argued in the previous section.

Fourth, the evolution of transnational production orchestrated exclusively, at least for much of the formative period of the process, by the giant corporations of the advanced industrial countries and of course with both the connivance and often the active involvement of their own governments, will almost inevitably lead to the extension of the forces of monopoly capitalism into countries and indeed continents, where it initially had a less secure footing. Increased infiltration of the institutions, mechanisms and ideas of monopoly capitalism will inevitably transform the nature of the newly industrializing countries. At such a point the intrusion may be seen as a dynamic and progressive force, and yet the seeds of stagnation are carried through into new territory and will ultimately grow and tend to dominate the progressive forces in the same way as in the older established industrial countries. Japan and, more recently, Korea and Taiwan are important cases where the progressive elements have been separated out from the potentially regressive elements via a process of control whereby new technology from outside has been adopted largely without foreign ownership. On the other hand, Singapore, whose economy is dominated by foreign transnationals, faced a serious problem in the early 1980s when their unit labour costs began to diverge significantly from those in less-developed countries (see the discussion in Chapter 1).

Thus, in the long term, we can expect that, as a result of the evolution of dominant transnationals and their spread across the world economy — almost without let-up or hindrance with the disintegration of state socialism — the general degree of monopoly in product markets will tend to rise, this rise will be spread across a greater fraction of the world economy, and as a result the underlying stagnationist tendency of monopoly capitalism will be enhanced.

Transnationalism also has a role in serving to sustain the tendency for the propensity to save to increase as the socialization of capital proceeds (Pitelis 1986). The growth of pension funds coupled with the growth in corporate retained earnings appears to have had a major impact in raising the ratio of aggregate savings to private disposable income (Marchanté 1987).[4] Given that an increasing propensity to save, by reducing aggregate demand, is likely eventually to raise the issue of the realization of profits in a world of monopoly capitalism, it may be argued that the whole process is likely to falter as profitable investment opportunities tend to dry up. This predicament, as Pitelis has argued, may be avoided by going transnational. Funds which might otherwise have been invested in the domestic economy, or not saved, will now be able to flow smoothly to foreign locations within the corporate organization, still serving the direct interests of those controlling such corporations. Thus the initial aim of gathering the savings of a broader spectrum of the population in order to allow corporate empires to grow can be sustained by extending the firm internationally as opportunities to invest domestically contract as a direct result of the effect of the whole process on domestic aggregate demand. Transnational flexibility serves to sustain a second stagnationist tendency — the long-term tendency for the propensity to save to increase.[5]

The impact of the two general tendencies to stagnation identified above, the one due to the increasing monopolization of product markets and the other due to the increasing socialization of capital through, for example, the 'pension funds revolution', will be accentuated by the associated political developments arising in a world where the power of the transnationals is growing. By acting generally to curtail the power of labour and the nation state in seeking to advance their own interests on the world stage, the élite that controls the transnationals is acting, via its strategic decisions, to contain forces which may otherwise tend to redistribute income away from profits. For example, while we might expect political democracy to create demands for the redistribution of income, wealth and power in favour of the majority, the existence of giant transnational centres of economic power will undermine such democratic demands as the locus of power shifts from democratically elected government. Similarly the efforts of organized labour to secure, via pressure on government, increases in the 'social wage' (for example, health and welfare benefits) and legislation of benefit to their members will also be undermined. The consequence is that whereas a stagnationist tendency could be averted by appropriate redistributions via the political process, which would tend to maintain aggregate demand, this will be rendered increasingly unlikely as a result of the increased political power provided by the transnational organization of production (see the discussion of 'divide and rule' in Chapter 4). The transnationals are increasingly an external force over which national governments have diminishing control, but to whom national governments are increasingly sensitive — see the later section on the issue of deindustrialization.

But the political process is also affected in another way. The existence of transnational corporations serves to reduce the effectiveness of the policies of the nation state when they are aimed at securing full employment. Keynesian demand management will prove less effective because of the greater leakage via imports induced by the transnational organization of production. Thus the incentive to adopt Keynesian policies will be weakened, whilst at the same time pressures to impose classical supply-side responses will increase. Deindustrialization, as will be seen later, would appear to require that real wages be reduced, and yet this change in itself would contribute to the stagnationist tendency induced by the redistributive processes already discussed. The overall effect, at the level of the world economy, is that the stagnationist tendency would be augmented by the general pressures to move away from Keynesian demand management and substitute policies requiring general wage-cutting. What may appear rational for one country, where investment is controlled by transnational organizations, will be collectively irrational, resulting in a downward spiral of falling demand and falling output and investment.

Supply-side explanations

We have examined two, complementary, demand-side explanations of stagnation, in both of which the recent development of transnationalism has a role. We now seek to establish that the emergence of such a stagnationist tendency within a specific country at a particular point in history may have a supply-side explanation. The first supply-side explanation relates to the interaction between transnational capital and organized labour (see Chapter 4) and the second to the expansion of unproductive activity within a certain type of advanced capitalism.

Transnationalism and deindustrialization

Associated with the evolution of the monopoly capitalist system over the first three-quarters of the twentieth century, with its growth of ever more dominant giant firms, was a parallel growth in the extent, power and militancy of organized labour within the advanced industrial countries. This in turn led to an accelerating wage–price spiral coupled with political developments that culminated in the growth of the 'social wage', that is, social expenditures where access is not regulated by market forces. Capital flight to other locations more conducive to capital accumulation tended to follow wherever conditions facilitated it. The present era, where production and markets are controlled by the élite of giant corporations with a transnational base and where national and international controls over trade and capital flows have been progressively reduced, provide those conditions. The combination of relatively unified international markets and giant international firms bestriding them provides a ready mechanism for the processes of deindustrialization to develop wherever the conditions for capitalist accumulation are weakened (see Cowling 1986).

In contrast to the earlier history of the development of monopolies and cartels around the turn of the century when protectionism was demanded, the present period is characterized by demands on the part of the transnationals for free trade (see Chapter 3) and the supranational institutions to pursue and sanction it: a global freedom to pursue accumulation, given their own dominance within the global system and given the threat, or potential threat, of organized labour and democratic politics at the level of the nation state. It is neo-imperialism of free trade in similar vein to the nineteenth century British imperialism of free trade (Krause and Ney 1975), but this time the imperialism is that of the transnationals. The latest manifestation of these demands is reflected in the role of the transnationals in pursuing the idea of the Single Market in Europe (see Ramsay 1990), and in NAFTA.

The new order has created a new international division of labour (see Chapter 4). The old international division of labour divided the world into the advanced industrial countries and the backward primary producers, with international trade between these groups of countries dominating world trade. With the evolution of the transnational corporation this simple dichotomy has been destroyed as industrial investment has been progressively shifted away from the advanced industrial countries to the unindustrialized or newly industrializing countries.[6] Corporate structures have evolved in ways that facilitate this process. Increasingly the major corporations are becoming coordinating agencies for large numbers of production units scattered round the globe, each supplying services to the dominant organization at competitive rates and paying competitive wages (see Chapter 3). This represents an extension of the notion of the multi-divisional corporation with its centralization of strategic, capital allocation decisions, coupled with the decentralization of operational production decisions. Now strategic marketing and production decisions are being added to the headquarters function, with small business in satellite relation with the dominant corporation. The dominant corporations' basic role is then to secure an allocation of production consistent with cost minimization, whilst maintaining or enhancing market control.

The generally observed tendency has been either towards subcontracting to other, usually smaller capitalist organizations (or even to individual households) at home or abroad, thus circumventing some of the difficulties giant organizations inevitably generate as a result of the growth in power of organized labour, or switching investment to new sites where labour is unorganized, has no history of large-scale organization, or has been cowed by a repressive regime. Such tendencies are manifest *within* as well as *between* countries — between the North-East and the South within the United States (see Norton 1986), as well as between the United States and Mexico or Hungary.[7] The central feature is an increasing geographical flexibility of capitalist production which has allowed capital to a considerable degree successfully to escape the clutches of organized labour within the advanced industrial countries and has thereby weakened considerably the position of labour in the areas of production that remain. As we have argued in earlier chapters, this has all been organized within a strategic decision-making structure organized by a corporate élite despite the resistance of others, whether labour or the wider community.

We have argued that the deindustrialization within the United States and Western Europe has come about as a consequence of the global strategy-making of the dominant transnationals with their origins within these economies. But there is a popular perception within the United States and Western Europe, promoted by a variety of political interests, that indeed a new international division of labour may have come about, but it has not been controlled by the giant corporations of the old order; rather, a new order prevails — that of the Japanese.[8] When analysing the relative performance of national economies this may appear to be the case: Japan increased its share of world industrial production and exports throughout the 1960s and 1970s, while the United States and Western Europe experienced declining shares. But if we measure changes in world sales classified by the nationality of the parent company, the advance of European industrial capital since 1967 exceeded that of Japanese industrial capital at least through to the early 1980s, being achieved by a relatively rapid expansion of foreign production, and US capital more or less held its own (Dowrick 1983). The conclusion must be that the deindustrialization experienced by the West as a whole in the 1970s and early 1980s cannot be ascribed to Japanese expansionism. The high relative growth rate of Japanese industrial capital in the 1960s took place in a period of relative buoyancy in economic activity in the West. It is clear that the forces of deindustrialization, which have been most obvious in Europe, have been most active during a period when European industrial capital was increasing its share of the world economy.

When considering deindustrialization in Europe, the experience of the British economy was an extreme one (see Blackaby 1979; Rowthorn and Wells 1987; Crafts 1991; Dicken 1992): there has been an absolute decline in manufacturing employment over an extended period (even in the 1960s when all the advanced industrial countries were experiencing an increase!) and a dramatic decline in international competitiveness — for the first time, the United Kingdom has become a net importer of manufactured goods. At the same time the United Kingdom stands out as second only to the United States in terms of overseas direct investment in the world economy. In 1960 the United Kingdom accounted for 18.3 per cent of the world total of outward direct investment, in contrast to 1.2 per cent for West Germany and 0.7 per cent for Japan! In 1985, despite a drop in share to 14.7 per cent, this was still well in excess of the much bigger and more successful economies of West Germany (8.4 per cent) and Japan (11.7 per cent). The evidence would support the view that the British economy entered a vicious circle of relative decline partly because of the special international connections of British capital, whereas in contrast the other Western European economies and Japan (see Chapter 1), largely exploiting foreign markets from a domestic production base, entered a virtuous circle of cumulative causation, with relatively high growth rates in output, investment, productivity growth and external demand. The response of the British government has been essentially deflationary, under the pressure of balance of payments and budget deficits, leading to a further deterioration in the underlying position. Thus whilst productivity growth in UK manufacturing in the 1980s increased significantly, the necessary investment required to secure a long-term improvement in competitiveness was not being made (Crafts 1991).

The direct evidence of the specific role of the transnationals in the deindustrialization of the British economy is limited, but supportive of the line of analysis we have advanced. Stopford and Turner (1985) report that, for their sample of fifty-eight British transnationals, the total domestic job loss over the 1972–83 period was 600,000, whereas jobs overseas went up by 200,000. Gaffikin and Nickson (1984) concluded that for ten major West Midlands-based transnationals domestic employment fell by 31 per cent over the period 1978–82, whilst overseas employment increased by 2 per cent over this period of deep recession. To get a more complete assessment of the impact of the transnationals we would need to calculate the knock-on effects of the domestic cutbacks on purely domestic firms and then proceed to compare the behaviour of the transnationals with national firms. But at the same time it would be wise to identify where the behaviour of national firms is itself largely determined by the strategic decisions of the transnationals, thus making them part of the transnationals, as we have sought to define them in the previous chapters.

The growth of unproductive activities

The second supply-side explanation of the development of stagnationist tendencies within monopoly capitalism relates to the growth of unproductive activities. As Wolff (1987) has put it: 'The forces of competition, which in the early stages of capitalism lead to rapid technical change and productivity growth, promote non-productive, and even counterproductive activities in its more advanced stages. The current stagnation in which much of advanced capitalism now finds itself thus appears to be rooted in one of the fundamental contradictions of the system'.

What are these unproductive activities? They are activities which serve to maintain, reproduce, or change an existing set of entitlements to the social product, and thus incorporate the functions of ruling, warfare, religion (as justification for an unequal social order) and the control of circulation. Whilst capitalism brought about a qualitative change in the disposition of the surplus, that is towards investment, nevertheless a contradictory force was set in motion involving the development of a complex exchange economy involving considerable unproductive expenditure. Within monopoly capitalism it has taken new forms: given that the imperative to accumulate is not so acute as in competitive capitalism, more resources were put into controlling the demand for the product, which had become more problematic with the development of mass production. Thus advertising in its broadest sense was expanded, together with new institutional arrangements for consumer credit. In addition, demand management to maintain the level of aggregate demand was inaugurated and expanded, as were military means for controlling overseas markets. Wolff's analysis of the United States reveals a dramatic expansion in unproductive output over the period 1947–58 (4.9 per cent p.a.), with the most rapid expansion within government, particularly defence and state and local expenditures, plus business and professional services (for example, advertising) — that is, militarism plus demand management at various levels. Subsequently, between 1958 and 1976, the growth rate slowed somewhat, to 3.9 per cent p.a., as federal government was cut back. Directly, or indirectly, this growth in unproductive activity absorbed *all* the increase in US employment over the period 1947–67. This, together with the poor rate of productivity growth within the unproductive sector itself (0.6 per cent p.a. over the 1947–76 period) implied a considerable reduction in the US productivity growth rate.

Wolff also found a strong inverse relation between unproductive activity and net capital formation: a crowding-out process with its roots in monopoly capitalism. Where the rate of growth of unproductive final demand exceeded that of total output (that is in the periods 1947–58 and 1967–76), the rate of net investment fell, and, conversely, when the unproductive growth rate fell below the total, the rate of net investment increased. From his supply-side perspective he views unproductive activity as socially irrational, given that it appears as a diversion from capital accumulation. He sees the stagnation of American capitalism in the 1970s and 1980s as related to its growth — to a historical decision taken by US capital to divert major resources to marketing, rather than to advance by technological growth as in the case of West Germany and Japan. This constitutes a differentiation of twentieth-century capitalisms which may have its roots in the reluctance by some national capitals to accept the mass-production paradigm, so that it is not so much the sale of a large and increasing volume of standardized products which is the central concern, but rather the continuing innovation of technically different products (Best 1990).

Of course, in static Keynesian terms unproductive expenditures are simply an ingredient in aggregate demand and in this sense appear socially rational within a system tending to stagnation — indeed, it was correctly argued by Rothschild (1942) that advertising had the particular virtue of stimulating demand whilst failing to create an increment in productive capacity which would pose the problem of finding a demand for its subsequent output! It is only from a dynamic, supply-side perspective that such expenditures appear socially irrational, and even from this perspective it remains unclear within the system of monopoly capitalism, as Rothschild anticipated. If it were possible that American capitalism, given its historical circumstances, could have followed the West German/Japanese route, stressing technological innovation rather than marketing, and if this route had yielded a superior level of economic welfare, then one may so conclude. But this seems almost to deny history. Simply holding back on these unproductive activities, like advertising, the law and war, does not in itself guarantee a more dynamic economy. It would appear that Wolff is addressing the symptoms of a deeper malaise whose cure has yet to be identified. We move to such matters in the final two chapters, where we argue that a deeper transformation of the monopoly capitalist system will be required to revitalize economies which have degenerated in the way Wolff describes.

A system without democratic planning

We turn now to those characteristics of the system of transnational production which feed in more directly to the processes of global stagnation, rather than indirectly through the redistribution of income, the socialization of capital, deindustrialization, the political process or the growth of unproductive activities. These characteristics all relate to the limitations of the private international planning of the allocation of production by the transnationals, on a sector-by-sector basis, within the world economy as a whole. For a much earlier, and very perceptive discussion, see Hymer (1972).

First, the additional flexibility offered by transnational organization implies greater instability due to more frequent relocation of production (connected with the processes of industrialization and deindustrialization) and therefore income and expenditure loss in a world with considerable frictions. Thus whilst the corporation is able to move production around the globe in a relatively frictionless way — indeed, it is structured, organized and operated to achieve this despite being inevitably constrained by a variety of economic, political and social processes — nevertheless this relatively frictionless adaptation *within* the corporation takes place within an economic environment where frictions are fundamental, being related to the locational rigidity of specific communities. The private system of planning is not itself confronted with the wider social costs of its own decisions. For countries (and regions) where production and investment are moving out, unemployment will inevitably rise and purchasing power will be lost, leading to a downward spiral in economic activity in general. The new international nomadism will contribute to the quantitative significance of this effect, but it is also the case that the frictions within the economic environments are not external to the economic system itself — they must be regarded, at least partly, as endogenous to the process of the transnational organization and reorganization of production.

It is obvious that there are many external frictions within the process of deindustrialization or reindustrialization such that labour, plant and equipment will not immediately be taken up by new firms, even in a situation where there is potential demand for such capacity. However, new production will often be averse to moving into regions or localities where old production has moved out because of the characteristics of the labour force (see Glyn and Rowthorn 1988 who identify pools of unemployment which fail to evaporate following rapid rates of deindustrialization in Western Europe). This may in part be that the skills or age of the labour force in question are inappropriate to the new production, for example, where manufacturing is being replaced by service sector employment, or an old form of technology by a new. But this is unlikely to be the whole explanation. For the same reason that production left, production will not readily be brought back: capital is seeking a malleable, unorganized, easily controlled group of workers and therefore prefers new, unorganized industrial workers in new areas, or perhaps women and young people in the older areas, being often new entrants to the labour market and therefore typically unorganized. None of this is meant to imply that there are categories of the labour force with certain skills highly prized by the corporation, but the observations of the international transmission of jobs by the transnationals over recent history strongly suggests that in the case of many occupations the switch of jobs to newly industrializing regions or countries faces no real impediments (Dicken 1992 offers comprehensive documentation).

This sort of response by employers usually means that workers becoming unemployed in the older industrialized areas have to move to the jobs rather than jobs being moved to the workers, at least until the reality or perception of the labour force in the older industrial areas being adequately cowed by long-term unemployment has been achieved. But moving workers to the jobs accentuates all the rigidities imposed by the social infrastructure. Forcing the migration of individual workers may contribute to the aims of the employer, but at great social cost: the speeding-up of the process of regional decline, plus all the adjustment costs imposed on the families involved, often effectively fatherless families. And yet the removal of the initial forces of stagnation becomes conditional on such disintegration: a dynamically inefficient social process has been inaugurated. Of course, as a consequence, other areas are being industrialized so that the net loss of income, as opposed to welfare, is determined by the output of workers in the industrializing regions prior to the switch in production, assuming the output of the product which is being relocated remains unchanged. Thus if unemployment is simply reallocated income losses will be minimized.

The second characteristic of the private transnational organization of production we focus on, which feeds in directly to the processes of global stagnation, is the form of integration of the international economy. The growth of international firms means that stagnationist tendencies generated in any one country, by any one or combination of the processes previously analysed, will be immediately transmitted across many countries, eventually leading to feedback on the originating country. The development of transnational production patterns will tend to speed up and amplify an international stagnationist tendency. Thus an integrated world economy is produced without an overall planning mechanism and yet with an international system of planning operating within each of its major constituent parts, the transnationals themselves, as recognized by Hymer (1972).[9] Thus rather than having the stability which could result from international integration within a supra-national planning agency operating at the macroeconomic level across national economies, we have the growing instability of international integration organized by individual transnational corporations.

The world financial system perhaps offers the most vivid example of the integration of the world economy within the capitalist system resulting in a heightened degree of instability. Over recent history, with increasing liberalization and the diffusion of advanced information technology, the system has become almost completely and immediately integrated. The outcome has been enormous instability induced by international currency speculation. The resulting huge short-term gyrations in exchange rates, in the 1980s and continuing in the 1990s, undermined the ability of industrial capitalism to plan its investment and production policies and make informed location decisions — the Japanese appear not to be overly influenced by these short-term fluctuations, being relatively long-termist in perspective, but the same cannot be said in other cases. Sharp cutbacks in investment in tradable goods because of the substantial increase in the degree of uncertainty surrounding such decisions appear to have been the consequence, and continue to be so. The central point is that the very flexibility of unregulated financial capital has impaired the efficiency of industrial capital. But clearly this is not a matter simply of flexibility, but one of unregulated flexibility: governments have little control over the process. The phenomenal growth of the Eurocurrency market decisively altered the balance of power, with international commercial banks emerging as a main focus of financial power, largely independent of the control of national monetary authorities (see Bhaduri and Steindl 1983).

At this point, the analysis points towards the conclusion that the growth in dominance of the transnational corporations over recent history may have accentuated stagnationist tendencies already endemic within monopoly capitalism. But has the case been overstated? Surely there is a positive side to the flexibility of the transnationals: surely flexibility is a good not a bad in terms of allowing the rapid adaptation of the world economy to new conditions? Surely also, these giant firms act in a beneficial way to innovate and diffuse new products and processes more rapidly through the world economic system?

On the first point, it is clear that a certain amount, and a certain type, of flexibility is going to be a good thing. Steindl (1966), for example, suggests that the existence of diversified giant corporations allows for the ready diversion of funds from monopolizing to competitive sectors of the economy, thus tending to sustain the rate of investment when otherwise we might expect it to fall, as argued earlier, but only to increase the degree of monopoly in the former competitive sectors. The significance of this process depends on the bounds of the system in terms of democratic control. Economics normally relates to nation states, in which case a sharp distinction has to be drawn between flexibility between monopolizing and competitive sectors *within* the nation state and flexibility *between* nation states. Thus the issue of the transnational and its flexibility appears qualitatively different from that of the purely national firm. But this has arisen because we have chosen to focus on the nation state. Similar issues arise for communities within nation states; for villages, towns, cities, regions, the optimality of the flexibility of giant firms takes on a very different meaning. Diversification of production within a community is likely to be desirable to provide a range of suitable employment opportunities and to act as an insurance against unexpected change, but the diversification of production within a typical transnational usually offers little in this regard.

We can respond to Scitovsky's (1980) comments on the flexibility or inflexibility of capitalism in a similar way. Contrary to our argument, and that of Steindl, Scitovsky suggests that capitalism is becoming more inflexible due to the increasing size and complexity of the firm, and this has resulted in a more fragmented economy — we are 'stuck with capitalism's unattractive features, but deprived of one of (its) great and redeeming virtues: its flexibility'. In terms of alertness to opportunities and ability to absorb shocks and adapt to changed circumstances, we would agree with Scitovsky — indeed in the concluding chapters we shall be arguing for a new organization of production which encapsulates these virtues. But this does not undermine what we have already said about both the creation of the transnational and its strategic thrust, which implies a locational flexibility quite unlike that of the small firm embedded within its local economy and community. Indeed, Scitovsky goes part way to recognizing the importance of the nature of flexibility when he states that 'there is something to be said in favour of inflexibility which locks in and isolates a fall in effective demand'.

Turning to the innovatory activity of the transnationals, it can readily be accepted that major innovations can serve to nullify stagnationist tendencies, either by reducing costs or stimulating demand (see, for example, Baran and Sweezy 1966) for an illuminating account of some of the major innovations of the (first two-thirds of the) twentieth century. Two questions arise: has the development of such innovations been enhanced by the growing dominance of the transnationals, and what is the nature of these innovations in a monopoly capitalist world? On the first point, the available evidence indicates that technological progressiveness will not normally be promoted by the monopolization of the system of production (see Scherer and Ross 1990 for a recent survey of the evidence). For example, a recent investigation of innovations in the United Kingdom over the period 1945–83 gives strong support to the view that innovatory activity has been retarded by high levels of concentration and restrictions on entry (Geroski and Stewart 1991). Despite controlling most of the recorded research and development, the giant corporations have not, in general, provided the origins of the major technological innovations. These are often appropriated from much smaller firms, or even individuals, and in many cases their innovation is suppressed or delayed (see, for example, Mandel 1968). However, the transnational organization of production does mean that once innovation takes place, then international diffusion should rapidly follow. In this sense transnationalism is a progressive force. But we must keep clear the purposes and consequences of such diffusion. The innovation of new products by these firms is an attempt to secure and enhance their market positions, and hence will contribute to the general tendency for the degree of monopoly to increase over time: innovation, whilst being a centrally important instrument of dynamic competition, is also a process whereby market concentration can be achieved and maintained. While in the short term such innovations may boost investment, in the longer term they can constitute a force contributing to the stagnationist trend.[10] It is similar with process innovations. Although those who control the transnationals will be motivated by the search for efficient techniques, this will include the 'efficiency' provided by control over the work-force. New technology will tend to reflect the search for control, which will inevitably have distributional implications: a bias in favour of replacing skill, via deskilling technologies, rather than enhancing skill by using the computer as an extension of human activity and creativity, will inevitably be present (see Council for Science and Society 1981). In addition there will be a bias embedded in the new technology favouring a system of production and control suited to the transnationals: if transnationality is seen to be an appropriate form of evolution for the giant corporation, then the enabling technologies of international communications, transportation and fragmentation of production will tend to be emphasized, rather than those technologies conducive to the local development of close networks of relatively small enterprises. Both biases will tend to sustain a stagnationist tendency, if our central arguments are accepted; to reverse it requires an accelerating rate of innovation providing a continuing and increasing short-term stimulus to investment, a requirement the system is ill suited to deliver.

Concluding remarks

Josef Steindl, stimulated by his earlier close association with Michal Kalecki, was the major originator of the line of analysis developed in this chapter. His path-breaking book, *Maturity and stagnation in American capitalism* (1952), was a remarkable achievement for its time, offering a powerful blend of theoretical and empirical analysis of a major event in the twentieth century history of the world economy, the Great Depression in its United States context.

However, quite recently, Steindl (1990) argued that his explanation of the stagnationist tendency of the first one-third of the twentieth century, in the case of the United States economy, could not be straightforwardly applied to that of the last one-third because of the rise in the power of labour and the growth of international competition. He also argued, in line with our own analysis, that 'the development and persistence of oligopolistic market structures over a long time cannot have been without effect on the internal structure, organisation and management of firms', which had in turn led to a greater emphasis on market control and a weakening of the incentive to invest. As a consequence of our examination of some aspects of the dynamic interactions between these features of the system, both in this chapter and earlier in the book, we conclude that the rise to dominance of the transnational organization of production within the modern giant firm, over the past thirty years or so, has at one and the same time created an intense international competition for jobs and eroded the disciplines of international competition in the product market by internalizing the processes and impact of international trade and production. Josef Steindl was too modest;[11] his explanation of the stagnationist tendency of the first third of the twentieth century remains highly applicable today, because firms have reorganized in the face of the dual threat that he described. At one level this is a depressing conclusion, but we do not have to accept the inevitability of the outcome. Within the terms of our analysis its inevitability lies only within the continuance of the monopoly capitalist system, but it is within our power to begin the transformation of the system and to move beyond capitalism. In the final two chapters we shall begin the construction of an alternative way forward, one which rejects the authoritarianism which characterizes both monopoly capitalism and state socialism, and offers in its place a much deeper democracy than we have yet experienced.

Notes

1 A fuller discussion of the arguments is available in Cowling (1982).
2 See, for example, Steindl (1952), Baran and Sweezy (1966), and Cowling (1982).
3 Neither the response of labour nor import competition is seen as capable of ultimately reversing this tendency.
4 There has of course been much discussion about the falling propensity to save in the 1980s. No doubt this has been linked to the freeing-up and indeed huge promotion of the credit-supplying industry. This has had a one-off impact rather than some continuing major effect on the underlying tendencies. The latest evidence points to a strong recovery in the propensity to save as people try to recover sustainable credit : income ratios.
5 Pitelis (1986, p. 103) records such a tendency for both contractual saving and personal saving from the early 1950s through to the late 1970s in the United Kingdom.
6 This is not meant to deny the growth of investment flows between the advanced industrial countries, but, to the extent to which this is symmetric, it offers no explanation of deindustrialization. Asymmetries can be due to differences on the demand side or on the supply side.
7 For a full and recent report on changing global patterns of production, see Dicken (1992).
8 This attitude has changed somewhat in recent years as the Japanese have switched from an export-oriented policy to one in which production within the United States and Western Europe by Japanese corporations has become much more important (for up-to-date details, see Dicken 1992). This has clearly been prompted by political tensions, but also by the significant increase in wage costs in Japan relative to other advanced industrial countries.
9 Of course, we have the market itself, but, as we have already argued, we do not see this as a self-regulating system creating the full employment of resources at the world level. Indeed, we see the market as very much the construction of the dominant corporations (see Chapter 6).
10 A fundamental distinction has to be drawn between product rivalry among the many and among the few. A rivalry that maintains deconcentrated structures has very different macroeconomic implications, but it may only be achieved within very specific institutional environments where such structures are secured by purposive public action (see the final two chapters).
11 It is a tremendous loss to our profession that Josef died last year.

Part III
THE WAY FORWARD

6

BUILDING A NEW ECONOMY: FOUNDATIONS[1]

At the beginning of the book we observed a world economy in some disarray as we approach the turn of the century. Not only do great masses of the world's population in the Third World suffer from extreme and unrelieved poverty, with little hope of anything better, but the conditions in Central and Eastern Europe and the former Soviet Union show a substantial worsening for the majority of the population, coupled with a growing feeling on their part that they will not see any significant improvement for many years. Finally, the advanced industrial countries show little propensity to secure full and well-paid employment for all their people: whilst poverty takes on a very different character in the Third World, there is nevertheless a real sense in which the condition of a significant and increasing minority of the population in these centres of wealth and power can only be described as poverty. The lack of economic performance, and the increasing inability to involve the full cross-section of society within the modern economy, point to a failure of the free market economy which cannot be remedied without a progressive transformation of the very structure of the system. That is the message of this book. Whilst much may be achieved in the relatively short term by a sufficient stimulus achieved by an expansionary demand-side policy, leaving the structure of the supply-side intact, such a policy will inevitably be revealed as incomplete unless accompanied by a supply-side transformation. An experiment of this sort was tried in Britain during the Lawson boom of the mid- to late 1980s and in the United States as a result of the fortuitous Keynesianism of the later Reagan years. The result was certainly expansion and a reduction in unemployment, but the growth required to bring about full employment was found to be unachievable. Large budget and trade deficits led to retreats from the expansionary policies of the earlier period and the early 1990s have as a result been a period of unremitting gloom. For those who believe that expansionary demand-side economic policies are sufficient to secure significant improvements in economic performance and full employment, the history of the late 1980s offers a cautionary tale. What was remarkable was not the huge budget and trade deficits that resulted, but rather that despite the significance of the demand-side expansion that resulted in such deficits, these economies still failed to generate growth sufficient to reabsorb an unemployed population that was created in the deep recession of the early 1980s. Whilst some will argue that if the expansion had been better managed a high and sustainable growth could have been achieved, they have still to demonstrate that full employment would have returned (see Kaletsky 1993). None of this is to deny that expansionary demand-side policies in the present conjuncture are necessary and will bring real gains, rather it is meant to emphasize that such policies are inevitably incomplete. For a sustainable level of growth to be achieved, sufficient to bring the economy to full employment and maintain that position, and at the same time secure a rate of productivity growth closer to the potential allowed by the full exploitation of science and technology, we contend that there has to be a supply-side transformation and this follows directly from an analysis of the reality of the free market economy.

The situation as it has developed this century is paradoxical. At one level, the free market economy has approached a more completely planned system as it has moved to its monopoly and transnational monopoly phase. Now we have central actors within the free market economy using the visible hand of corporate strategy-making to achieve, from their own point of view, an efficient allocation of resources at the level of the world economy. Writ large, a relatively few transnational corporations have provided an international planning mechanism for the world economy capable of responding smoothly and flexibly to the world markets' ever-changing needs. Surely the institutions of capitalism have responded to the changing opportunities offered to the free market economy by developments in the facilitating technologies of transportation, communications and organization to bring to everyone, rapidly and efficiently, the fruits of the world's production system. There has been much reporting in recent years of the contrasts between the content of retailing outlets in the formerly centrally 'planned' economies and those of the advanced capitalist economies. Whilst the differences were real enough, to presume from the observed content of Western supermarkets the optimality of the organization of world production would seem wide of the mark. Even if their content were considered entirely appropriate and desirable, there can be no presumption that a very differently structured food industry could still continue to provide those same goods, and there could be other goods which might only appear or reappear where the production and retailing system were based on smaller-scale operations. For example, it is often remarked that large-scale retailing chains, with their highly centralized strategy-making, reflect very little of the region within which they are located — you may be in the middle of apple-growing country in the United Kingdom but the apples offered are still restricted to the standard international fare.

Thus an international planning mechanism which is operated in a way that is congruent with corporate interests, despite all its undoubted sophistication, cannot be presumed to be appropriate to the needs of the strategic planning of the economic future of local, regional or national communities. Indeed, even at the supranational level, for example, the European Union, or various constructions of a Greater Europe, the same principle applies: meeting the long-term objectives of geographical communities, at whatever level might be appropriate, cannot be achieved with world-wide planning mechanisms and institutions, controlled by a very limited segment of the population, unaccountable to the rest of society, and focusing, despite their scale, on only one segment of the total economy. There appear to be three types of systemic deficiencies:

— the breadth and depth of *participation* within the decision-making structure
— the width of the *sector* for which strategic decisions are being made
— the *geographical space* over which strategic decisions are being made

but the fundamental deficiency is the first. If full participation is achieved then the appropriate width of sector or geographical space becomes a matter of design. Without participation we cannot presume that the other systemic deficiencies will be resolved: the strategic decisions will reflect the interests of the controlling group rather than the community at large.

To illustrate, consider the question of monocultures, that is the specialization of a particular locality, region or country in a very narrow range of economic activity, whether it be steel, motor car assembly or sugar. This lack of sectoral and occupational breadth is often seen to be undesirable, and particularly so when control spans many localities, regions or countries. But it is clear that a fully participative decision structure would not give rise to monoculture — a community would perceive that such a structure of production would unnecessarily inhibit the full development of the community: different people within the community have different talents and interests and require a diversity of occupational opportunity sufficient to meet their varied requirements.

But we are running ahead of ourselves. From the description and explanation of the world economy in crisis we have offered in this book we now seek to piece together a way forward. We propose to do this quite carefully and in a step-by-step fashion because we are treading quite unfamiliar territory. The seeds of our proposals have already been planted in the earlier chapters, but we now need to thread together these arguments and distil from them the essence of the necessary changes we have to make in the way we organize the economy and society in order to escape our current predicament. We start by identifying a gap in policy-making which appears quite general over recent history — the absence of an industrial strategy. We then proceed to establish the guiding principles for the development of a strategy aimed at the evolution of a world economy both reflecting and nourishing the pursuit of the general well-being (Sen 1993). These guiding principles through which we identify an appropriate set of economic and industrial policies we now turn to. We shall subsequently, in the final chapter, illustrate these principles by reference to the central and topical issues of privatization, inward investment, technology policy, Europe and the regions, and finally to the activities of the IMF/World Bank axis. The book will end with an attempt to draw together the threads of our analysis and proposals.

The policy gap

It is our contention that the condition of the world economy today warrants the radical restructuring and reorganization of its industrial base to such a degree that the fundamental basis of the market system will be transformed from what is often referred to as the free market system to one that can be accurately described as a democratic market economy. This is not to imply that the measures we advocate are designed to bring about an overnight transformation, but rather that they are aimed at initiating a process of change whose inevitable consequences, if pushed through to their logical end, will be revolutionary. It is, of course, possible to engage in policy-making aimed at a less dramatic transformation but where gains to the general welfare could be substantial — expansionary, demand-side policies would be a case in point — but it is our view that inevitable contradictions will reappear. Such policies address only the symptoms of a deeper malaise: the patient will experience real relief from the treatment, but the illness remains and without more radical and holistic treatment will continue to undermine the patient's general well-being.

But have we not seen governments recognizing the deficiencies of the free market and reacting to them with a variety of industrial and economic policies? Indeed, we have; there has been no shortage of policies on trial at various times and in various places. Nevertheless, we would argue that economic policy-making in Western Europe and the United States, at least in the twentieth century, and currently in Central and Eastern Europe and the former Soviet Union together with much of the South, is characterized by the absence of a coherent industrial strategy. As industrial issues arise, for example, the Japanese challenge as perceived by the United States and Western Europe in the case of automobiles, electronics and areas of the communications industry, it becomes clear that although nation states, with certain important exceptions that we shall address later, have a variety of industrial policies, nevertheless they generally lack an overall strategy for industrial development. There is nothing that is coherent and consistent; not even *laissez-faire*.

Partly because of this vacuum in policy-making, as issues come to the boil the debate tends to become polarized in such a way that more positive, and potentially creative approaches tend not to command serious attention. On the one side those who believe in unadulterated market forces argue that these issues represent normal adjustments to the international forces of economic development. Nation states or communities should not intervene as doing so would delay a completely natural process of evolution which leaves everyone ultimately better off: the domestic automobile industry, for example, is allowed to succumb to these forces, if that is what they dictate. These issues are seen to reflect the working-through of essentially progressive forces, flexibly moving resources into better uses. Some may wonder at the extensive nature of under-used resources within this flexibly adjusting world, but the argument would be that this is a necessary short-term concomitant of these long-term processes: it cannot be avoided and to attempt to do so would be a misguided venture which would ultimately imply further dislocation.

On the other side are those whose knee-jerk reaction is to demand government action to stop whatever is happening, to preserve the *status quo*, to argue that it is cheaper to keep people at work than pay out public funds to maintain them in idleness. In terms of the above example, the automobile industry is allowed to ossify, with new ideas firmly excluded. This is the preservationist position (see Norton 1986): if we once get involved in a particular economic activity, then that activity should be preserved. Not to do so would be wasteful of skills, of people, of community.

Between these two poles there are many shades of opinion, but alternative views relating to industrial policy are being crowded out by the siren voices coming from the entrenched extremes of this axis. Our view is that there are elements which are valid in both lines of argument, but what is missing from both is an appreciation that government's role can be anything more than either preserving the rules by which market forces are allowed their full expression or maintaining the activities that market forces have already deemed appropriate for a particular community. Both positions are in this sense innately conservative. A more creative, proactive role for government and more fundamentally for community within the economic sphere is a dimension which is not articulated, not even recognized.

The essential thrust of this chapter is to develop the basis and explore the implications of a creative, proactive approach to economic and industrial strategy, given the mounting evidence of an economic system in deep disarray. Bearing in mind that some economies have managed to maintain a substantial degree of independence from the crisis enveloping the majority, it would seem clear that we have much to learn from their experience, and indeed we shall examine the nature of policy and its impact in the case of Japan, other Pacific Rim economies, and the Third Italy. However, we will go beyond advocating mere imitation of others' success. Indeed, rather than founding our analysis primarily on recent experiences of policy-making, we will build an argument essentially based on our analysis of the nature and behaviour of the major corporations which dominate the world economy. The approach we advocate seeks to address industrial issues *before* they boil up as specific, headline-grabbing problems demanding immediate and inevitably poorly thought-out attention. This does not presume omniscience, but a willingness to get involved in the strategy-making of the major actors within the economy and an involvement in constructing a framework within which their decisions will be made. Unlike traditional approaches, the basis for our proposals is not an analysis which starts with markets and the consideration of market failure. For us, industrial policy is not essentially about markets. Rather, we start with deeper and more fundamental concerns, building a policy perspective which recognizes that markets have a role as an important instrument of economic development, but that they are only an instrument. We root our analysis in the socially incomplete nature of strategic decision-making in modern corporations. We identify strategic planning of industrial activity as the key issue of industrial development and thus advocate strategic planning by communities as the core issue for industrial policy.

What seems to be missing in traditional approaches, at least within Western capitalism in the twentieth century, is any broad overarching debate about the sort of economy we wish to see created, coupled to an assessment of how such an objective can be realized. Those believing in the market are quite happy with whatever is thrown up; they have no particular views about what it should or might be like. Those believing in preserving particular structures appear to be saying that nothing better is possible. These alternatives would appear to offer a very restricted vision. Should communities be dictated to by the 'impersonal' (or not so impersonal) forces of the market? Should they be dictated to exclusively by their past, which many would accept was one they would not wish to repeat? This is not the way the dominant economic organizations of the market see themselves and their future, as we have tried to demonstrate in this book. The large corporations plan for their long-term future within the market — an activity represented as corporate strategy and one supported by the enormous expansion in business education throughout the West over the past thirty years. But we should be clear that corporate strategy does not constitute any form of industrial strategy. More specifically corporate strategy-making encapsulates the ambitions of those who control the major corporations, which in aggregate do not constitute the collective ambitions of nations or regions. And it is clear that a market system dominated by such corporate strategy-making cannot be relied on to achieve a correspondence between the two. Is it not therefore logical that communities should begin the construction of their own strategies? It should appear as natural as corporate strategy-making and it justifies at least equal attention within public education as does corporate strategy-making in the business schools. Indeed, whilst corporate strategy is not industrial strategy, many of the concepts and techniques can be adapted to form an important input into the development and implementation of community strategy, but their successful adaptation requires us to be clear about the guiding principles of industrial strategy-making and it is to those principles that we now turn.

Guiding principles

If industrial policies for nations or regions are to be successful not by luck but by judgement, their design needs to be grounded in theoretical and empirical analysis explaining industrial activity: the theory and empirics should lead to the policies — industrial strategy cannot be defined in a vacuum. Recognizing the crucial nature of such a link we now seek to outline a basis for industrial strategy which is informed by the analysis of the contemporary reality of the free market system which has been developed within the book; in doing so we will recap, generalize and extend our analysis in Chapters 2 to 5. We aim to establish a clear and logical link between our analysis of the deficiencies of the present system of monopoly capitalism and appropriate remedies. Rather than offering a magpie-like collection of specific devices aimed at securing better performance within small facets of the total economy, we aim to offer a systemic approach which constitutes a cohesive set of policies which can be reasonably represented as an industrial strategy and which has some general applicability to issues of industrial development.

Socially incomplete decision structures

In a so-called free market economy the distribution and allocation of resources is essentially determined by the interplay of various actors, for example, individuals, households and firms, operating within a set of ground rules implemented and policed by the state. A popular perception is that such a system yields optimal results and a well-recognized, although now qualified theoretical conclusion is that a complete set of perfectly competitive markets yields a Pareto-efficient outcome: resources cannot be reallocated without someone being worse off. However, equally important but far less recognized is the idea of an even distribution of power. This is seen in the voluntary exchange concept, a tenet of mainstream economics (neo-classicism) that gives everyone the right of veto, and no one the power to force another into a worse position.

The reality of the free market economy, however, is that the markets and institutions acting within it are manipulated by a powerful subset of the population. These élite influence situations and events for their own benefit and hence observed outcomes will be optimal for some but not for society as a whole. As a consequence a free market economy is a socially inefficient economy. This is not a problem of markets *per se*, rather a problem with the way markets are used. Underlying this analysis is a view, and a theory, of the firm that does not begin with markets; rather we see markets as rooted in organizations (for a fuller treatment of this perspective see Cowling and Sugden 1993c). The analysis of monopoly capitalism, specifically within its present transnational phase, contained in this book points clearly in this direction. This is quite different to widely accepted approaches. When looking at the essence of the firm, its overall nature and what it is, mainstream economists' thinking essentially goes back to Coase (1937), Alchian and Demsetz (1972), and Williamson (1975, 1985). All of these start with markets. Our concern is to analyse from strategic decision-making to the theory of the firm and the use of markets. We see the firm as essentially about strategic decision-making, not about markets (see Chapter 2).

Consider, for instance, the structure and activities of a typical large Anglo-American corporation.[2] Decisions within such a firm can be classified into three types: decisions made by individuals about their own work; tactical, day-to-day, operational decisions; and strategic decisions, concerning broad corporate objectives. All three categories of decision determine what actually happens in production, but the strategic decisions are especially significant because, by definition, they essentially determine the direction of the firm. Moreover, the linkages between the three types are dominated by a hierarchy and, the further up the hierarchy, the fewer the number of people involved in making the decision. Different people play different roles in the decision-making process. Everyone in a firm makes working decisions, which are severely constrained by both strategic and operational decisions. In contrast, only managers make operational decisions, albeit from a set of options largely determined by strategic decisions. Most importantly, the latter are made by an élite, despite resistance from others. Some managerialists argue that the élite are senior managers, others that they comprise major shareholders, others that these two groups are effectively the same set of people anyway. Whatever the opinions may be, almost all but the purest neo-classical economists would accept that strategic decisions are effectively made by a subset of those involved in a firm. These strategic decision-makers take the firm in directions which they prefer rather than in directions others would like to follow.

The consequences of this are far-reaching, as we have suggested in Chapters 2 to 5. For instance, it is commonly argued that senior managers seek maximum profits. If it is assumed they control firms, we should therefore expect firms to aim for product market monopolization with all its implications for allocative efficiency, income distribution and stagnation. Consequently we should expect firms to manipulate markets by colluding, because this will suit the interests of those making strategic decisions. It may not suit others in society, for instance, people seeking jobs or consumers seeking low prices, but it will suit strategic decision-makers. Indeed, this illustration is especially pertinent because a mainstream (neo-classical) alternative to our characterization is that appropriate market competition would remove any tendency for strategic decision-makers to impose their will. In the product market, for example, it could be argued that price competition amongst sellers would ensure that each can obtain only normal profits: any excess will be washed away, at least in the long run, by the processes of competition. However, this misses the point. Profit-seeking firms will avoid price competition that implies normal profits precisely because it implies normal profits.

Similarly, when decisions are being made about a firm's geographical development we should expect those decisions to be made in the interest of profit and nothing else. Thus when conditions for accumulation weaken in any particular country, we should not be surprised to see deindustrialization and hence unemployment. Strategic decision-makers will aim to ensure that a firm locates production where conditions for accumulation are optimal. Shop-floor workers may object, as may deserted communities, but neither is making the crucial decisions.

Thus concentrated decision-making power in a free market economy results in an élite planning for their own benefit, without regard to the costs imposed on others. Because of the roles different people play, such an economy is necessarily inefficient. The systematic consequences of opting for a free market economy have been explored throughout this book and it is interesting to observe that the United States and Britain — the closest to mature, free market economies that can be observed in practice — have revealed a relatively poor performance over the last half-century; perhaps this is some indication of the price we pay for free markets! We suggest that the consequences for people's well-being of concentrated decision-making power can in fact be grouped into three sets of interrelated systemic deficiencies: transnationalism, centripetalism and short-termism.

Transnationalism is the main focus of our analysis throughout this book. The growth in dominance of the transnational corporation poses a significant potential threat for any national market economy. The global perspective and ambitions of the major industrial and financial corporations, with their present almost ubiquitous transnational base in terms of control if not direct ownership, may cut across the interests of any particular nation state, or any particular community, whether or not such corporations have their origins in that nation or community, or some other. The fundamental issue relates to the asymmetry of power between corporation and community, which derives from the transnationality of the corporation — and the international perspective and flexibility which that implies — compared with the inherent locational rigidity of a specific local, regional and national community. We have seen in Chapter 4 that divide-and-rule strategies can be used to achieve lower labour costs; there is widespread evidence that transnationals play off both workers and governments in different countries to increase profits. To achieve its own objectives the transnational can switch investment and production, or threaten to do so, whenever conditions in any one country or region appear disadvantageous, for example, because wage costs or profit taxes are too high. Thus any one nation can be deindustrialized by the actions of transnational corporations, and the implication is that only when wage costs are cut, or profit taxes reduced, will capital return. Thus transnationals which are left 'free' can impose their strategies on communities. To protect itself, any community has to intervene in the strategy-making, or accept their dominance in its own affairs. To do so is to admit that a nation or community has no real autonomy.

The issue of transnationalism is a perfectly general phenomenon. That is, without intervention, we are involved in a negative-sum game (Chapter 5): national communities in general can suffer from the unrestricted activities of the transnationals. Any community considering a tax or wage increase will be faced with the possibility that capital will migrate in response. The general, system effect is that wages and taxes on profits will be held down against the wishes of each national community, and, similarly, subsidies to investment or production will be raised above what they might otherwise have been. Conservative administrations, as we have witnessed recently in both Britain and Germany, in making these arguments are absolutely right — up to a point. Within the context of free market economies this is the inevitable outcome at some stage of development. Where these administrations are wrong is in conceding, or indeed promoting, the inevitability of the free market system and its superiority to any feasible alternative; we cannot escape its consequences unless and until radical measures are taken that will eventually bring about a transformation in the system.

Thus we have a basis for recommending international regulation of the transnationals, a matter for both West and East as transnationals seek to extend their activities into the centrally planned economies; but it is also a basis for establishing a role for community-based industrial strategy-making. We need a framework of strategic planning within which to position the transnationals. We need to approach them, and bargain with them, within the context of such a strategy, otherwise their strategy will inevitably become our strategy without our having had any voice in the process. The transnationals are not a threat if their strategies are harmonized with the national economic strategy, but a necessary condition for such harmonization is the existence of a national economic strategy. Having established such a strategy, cultural, political and economic pressure will be required to ensure that harmony is achieved and maintained. There can be no doubt that this is a major political project. However, by clearly identifying fundamental deficiencies in the free market system dominated by the transnationals we are aiming not only to specify what is politically desirable but also to help make it politically feasible. Our view is that the balance of political forces is affected by the development of analysis and ideas within the context of changing economic forces.

Centripetalism is a closely related deficiency of free market systems; in Chapter 3 we suggested that transnationals' influence implies centripetalism as a systemic feature of the international economy, but it is also more generally a deficiency that needs to be addressed. It relates to the tendency for higher-level economic, political, social and cultural activities to gravitate to the centre — to be lost to the regions, to be lost to the periphery. At the international level the phenomenon is explored most forcefully by Hymer (1972). He argued that a vertical division of labour within firms would produce a corresponding hierarchical division of labour between geographical regions. Thus amongst transnationals strategic decision-making is concentrated in a handful of major cities of the world. At one and the same time the major corporations are internationalizing production and drawing the control of the use of an ever-increasing share of the world's economic resources into the ambit of the key cities of the world — cities like New York, Tokyo, London, Paris. Feagin and Smith (1987) refer to

such cities as world command cities containing '... extraordinary concentrations of top corporate decision-makers representing financial,
industrial, commercial law and media corporations'. These cities are
the centres of dominant economic power. They are the major concentrations of income and wealth, and attract the best doctors, lawyers,
artists and entertainers. Moreover, strategic decision-making in other
firms serving transnationals and transnational employees is concentrated in particular cities, reflecting transnationals' uneven spread. In
part this is due to decision-makers choosing to enjoy the better standard of living available (for them) in this subset of the world's major
cities.

The transformation lying behind the current situation has led to the
loss of a substantial degree of local, regional and national autonomy.
And this is not only reflected in the ambit of the major corporations as
defined by ownership. The control of such giants extends well
beyond their legal bounds into most of their subcontracting, agency
and franchise relationships (Chapter 2). The result is that strategic
decisions with major implications for many local, regional and
national communities are being taken outside those communities.
The siphoning-off of resources to the centre reduces the capacity of
the periphery to sustain its own economic, political and cultural
development, which inevitably leads to outmigration of the educated
and thus further decline. It is for this reason that investing in education cannot easily retrieve the position unless parallel action is taken
to secure strategic control of production and investment more generally.

The systemic short-termism of the free market system, the third
major deficiency we focus on, is in turn related to the other two we
have already described. Short-termism is related to transnationalism
within the context of any one nation, region or community since the
transnational has only a limited commitment to it in the long term as
a location for production (see Chapter 3). The case is similar for centripetalism. The withdrawal of strategic decision-making from the
periphery will extend the infection of short-termism. Whilst the
centre, the key city location, will be taken as a relatively fixed point,
the periphery, the regions, will be viewed in a different light. For
example, whilst the cultural dynamism of a city may have important
long-term consequences for its economic dynamism, for example, in
terms of attracting and keeping a variety of talents, this may elicit
little response from strategic decision-makers located elsewhere. The
interrelated growth of the forces of transnationalism and centripetalism implies an increasing failure to internalize various

dynamic external economies. Whereas locally based industry could recognize the economic importance for them of 'cultural' investment — witness the way in which, for example, institutions of further and higher education have been initiated and funded by local industry — this link has been substantially broken. Industrial funding may be still there, but it is no longer core funding nor institutionally innovative, rather it is peripheral to the publicly and centrally provided core.

The organizational forms and institutions of the modern corporate sector, which reflect the needs of the transnational, centripetal developments we observe, may also act to promote a short-termist view. In this respect the advent of the multi-divisional (M-form) corporation is interesting (see, for example, Williamson 1970). Hymer (1972) identifies the importance of this organizational form as an enabling condition in the development of the giant transnational corporation but also in the development of firms more generally. However, the M-form incorporates some of the seeds of short-termism within its structure. Profit centres (product or geographical divisions) are forced into short-term, profit-maximizing stances to justify being allocated capital for further investment, and thereby fail to take the long-term strategic aims of the corporation fully into account. Thus whilst the M-form corporation may be efficient in enforcing short-run, cost-minimising behaviour and in securing an unbiased strategic posture for the corporation as a whole, there remain questions concerning the efficient implementation of long-term strategy within divisions, and more fundamentally about the appropriateness of the centralization of long-term strategy (see Porter 1987).

One explanation of the spread of the M-form structure sees it as an attempt to introduce the discipline of the financial markets within the corporate structure, where outside it the external financial markets are constrained by their lack of adequate information, and yet it is the financial institutions themselves that are often regarded by industry as excessively short-termist. This particular aspect of short-termism will vary in importance from country to country as the structure and strategy of the financial institutions vary, with Britain and the United States perhaps suffering most, given the lack of direct involvement of the banks in industry via equity or long-term loans, and with Germany and Japan at the other extreme, with their banks being more closely tied to industry (Jenkinson and Mayer 1992). But it remains the case that for most market economies the question of short-termism is likely to loom large. What this means is that incremental change can be handled quite well, but more fundamental changes involving quantum leaps in product, process or structure and therefore requiring an extended period of time for their fulfilment, will not be handled so well.

Nevertheless, the financial institutions can only impose their short-term perspectives on industry via those firms incapable of raising finance internally. Thus new and small firms may be severely constrained in their investment ambitions, whereas by contrast the bigger, established corporations will retain a significant autonomy. However, an active market in the control of existing corporations via acquisition could overturn all that. Such a market for corporate control allows the short-term perspective of the financial institutions to impinge much more decisively on the perspective of industry. Again, the position in different countries markedly varies, as we indicated in Chapter 3; whilst a market for corporate control is highly developed and active in the United States and Britain, it scarcely exists in Germany and Japan (Charkham 1989). But more and more of the institutions and mechanisms of the 'efficient' financial markets of the United States are being considered for adoption by countries not so well endowed and as a result we might expect to observe the extension of a financial environment which is hardly conducive to the rational planning of the long-term future of the industrial base. Short-term decision-making is crowding out long-term issues.

However, whilst we can readily agree that short-termism has become an issue within the free market economy, and is indeed most clearly manifest in the most advanced forms of such economic systems, our central concern is with the extent to which the time horizon of decision-making within the socially incomplete decision structures of the free market economy fails to coincide with the broader community interest. By its very nature a particular community may be especially concerned with its long-term position and development; it has a vested interest in seeing that the location it occupies thrives and prospers into the future. However, its basic difficulty is that the strategic decision-making of firms is based on the wishes of an élite, not on the wishes of the community. This may cause problems because the élite pursues short-term objectives, by choice or otherwise, as we have inferred in our earlier discussion. More to the point, however, whether firms in a free market system plan short term or long term, they do so in the pursuit of their strategic decision-makers' wishes. This is in no sense long-term planning for the communities in which they do or do not operate. This issue is particularly significant where firms are transnationals with global strategies but is more generally the case. The point is starkly illustrated by the deindustrialization argument. It was suggested earlier that transnationals' strategic decision-makers will ensure that production activity will be located in whichever country a firm can obtain the highest profit. They have no particular commitment to a specific location, in contrast to the inhabitants of particular areas. More generally, the strategic decision-makers of a firm which spans one country but not several have no particular commitment to specific locations within that country.

Thus we see transnationalism, centripetalism and short-termism as interrelated and systemic deficiencies that are inherent features of a free market economy. The very nature of the system implies their presence; a free market economy cannot avoid problems associated with monopolization, deindustrialization and constrained technological change because these are essential features of the system. The crucial, strategic planning role within a firm is deliberately assigned to an élite who are not only given powers to pursue their own interests; they are actually encouraged and expected to do so. Thus we should not be surprised to observe monopolization and deindustrialization; the surprise would be if they were absent! Moreover, an implication of our analysis is that most people in society are channelled into roles that suit élite strategic decision-makers. Not only are they denied involvement in strategic decision-making, itself a direct stifling of their talents and abilities; they are conducted into activities that are severely constrained by the strategic decisions of others. Hence a free market economy suppresses personal development. It is an economy where human resources in general are neither cultivated nor utilized for the full benefit of either individuals in general or of communities. Of course, it is argued by some that participation is ruled out by 'the facts of economic life' — the problems posed by scale in modern industrial society and the apathy, lack of knowledge, and indeed alienation of the individual. But we would wish to turn this sort of argument on its head. If scale raises problems for effective participation, and yet we regard participation as crucial, then either we need to design participative structures which allow problems of scale to be surmounted, or industrial structures which reduce the significance of scale. Similarly, the 'fact' of apathy, lack of knowledge and alienation is not an argument against participation, but for it (see the illuminating discussion in Lively 1975, pp. 85–7). The greater the participation of the individual, the better able she is to do so.

The focus of our concerns with the socially incomplete decision structures of free market economies has tended to emphasize the production side of the economy without recognizing fully the endogenous nature of the pattern of consumption (see, for instance, Cowling and Naylor 1992). But we would argue that within a capitalist economy the choice set open to the individual, as a consumer as well as a producer, is itself constrained to be compatible with the reproduction of the social relations of that system; that is, it is constrained to be congruent with the aims and ambitions of the élite group controlling the strategic decision-making of the major corporations. Thus, whilst the orthodox view of the free market economy has the producer, for instance, the major corporation, responding to the expressed desires of the individual via the market, we would see the wants to which capitalist production is responding are, at least in part, determined directly or indirectly within the capitalist system of product. Then the whole structure of the system is invertible. Whilst in the new sequence the individual continues to maximise her utility, adjustments can be brought about just as easily by the manipulation of preferences as by the reallocation of budget or time by the individual. Once this sort of intervention by powerful producers is admitted, then the case against other forms of intervention in the microeconomics of the system of consumption is no longer as clear as the economic orthodoxy would have us believe. If we are to allow corporate strategy-makers the freedom to constrain and persuade, that is, the freedom to decide what is to be produced and to encourage us to buy in order to mesh predetermined production with consumption, then we cannot fairly disallow a role for democratic agencies in shaping choices facing the individual: the notion of a socially incomplete decision structure extends to the sphere of consumption and implies similar inefficiencies. Even where individuals are allowed to exercise their decision-making power as consumers this will not secure a welfare optimum because the preferences and choice set available are to some degree determined or constrained by the system itself. Allocative efficiency requires both producer, in the sense of individuals as workers, and consumer sovereignty; the apparent paradox is resolved by recognizing the individual as both producer and consumer, and that sovereignty relates to different levels of decision-making. On both sides, production and consumption, it is also crucial to recognize that individuals can realize their ambitions only by acting collectively, given the nature of both consumption and production. More on this later.

We have argued earlier that the issue of socially incomplete decision structures as it relates to production looms largest within monopoly capitalism. This is true also on the consumption side. This is perhaps most evident in terms of the manipulation of preferences, since the enormous growth of the advertising industry and the increasing concentration of the communications industry have been central characteristics of the growth of monopoly capitalism. Fewer and fewer people are dominating an increasingly intrusive system of communications with an increasingly powerful and all-pervading commercial message. Perhaps less obviously the increasing concentration of control over economic resources implies a tendency towards a narrowing in the choice set offered to consumers. Of course, the message of the media stresses the dramatic increase in choice, but closer examination typically reveals this description to be quite spurious. Investment in minimal product differentiation is substantial, but the provision of real choice seems increasingly circumscribed. This argument should not be pushed too far because worthwhile innovations are constantly being made. The concern is that these innovations cluster along a line of development which may have little correspondence with that sought by specific communities, and that the increasing concentration of control of the use of resources will serve to minimize the degree of experimentation in the provision of real alternatives. As well as raising issues of monopolization and deindustrialization by limiting the involvement of people in strategic decision-making, the free market economy serves also to restrict people's experiences on the consumption side as consumer sovereignty is replaced by the sovereignty of those directing the strategy-making of the major corporations. The joint impact of these two elements of socially incomplete decision-making serves even more decisively to suppress personal development within a free market economy, since the advance of the ambit of corporate control will inevitably constrain the range of experiences that communities would otherwise choose to offer. The present moves to commercialize and/or privatize public broadcasting in Britain is an important case in point. Not only has the impact of the BBC been felt by way of its own offerings, but its very presence has inevitably changed the nature of what is offered outside the BBC. To remove the BBC, in one way or the other, can be expected to precipitate a sharp narrowing of the broadcasting experiences on offer.

Democratic decision-making

Faced by these deficiencies of the free market system, an obvious response is to address the most fundamental cause for concern. The basic argument is very simple. A firm in which strategic decisions are taken by a subset of the population will serve the interests of that subset. Accordingly, a firm can only serve the interests of a community more widely if more of the community's people are involved in making strategic decisions, that is only if there is greater democracy. A prime task for economists is to design policies by which communities are represented in the process of strategic decision-making within the economy.

We are reluctant to be too precise about what is meant by the term community. A community is one of those things that people know when they see it, and a precise definition would be hard, perhaps impossible to provide — there is a risk of becoming bogged down in an unnecessary definitional debate. Nevertheless, in exploring the meaning an obvious route is via the sociological concept of 'connectedness' (closely linked networks of personal relationships; see Frank 1992). A community is essentially concerned with linkages between individuals, but it is important to observe that there are various sorts of community and that they often overlap in their composition.

Underlying our analysis is the view that the members of a community are generally capable of collectively deciding for themselves what best satisfies their objectives, and the active process of participation will, in itself, inevitably improve their ability to do so (Lively 1975); making mistakes is part of the process of learning, and is anyway preferable to the dictatorship of some other group. What this means in terms of growth and many other indicators of economic performance which economists use is in one sense irrelevant. If communities can generally make decisions best suiting their objectives, the observed outcome should generally be in line with what communities seek. Having said this it seems reasonable to suggest that wealth creation is an important determinant of welfare: it provides communities with the means of achieving a range of broader objectives (Sugden 1990). Hence the logic of our argument is to expect community control generally to imply successful wealth creation — increased productive efficiency and growth, taking fully into account the community costs of the pursuit of these objectives. There is considerable empirical support for this implication (see, for instance, Thomas's 1982 analysis of production in the Mondragon region of Spain). The region has a large cooperative sector in which the work-force has a considerable say over its own activity. Yet the cooperatives are 'more productive and more profitable' than conventional firms where decision-making is dominated by an élite few; for a more general assessment of cooperative production see Stewart (1983).

Precisely how we might move in the direction of a more democratic economy, given where we find ourselves today, needs detailed attention and imagination. Obviously this does not imply that everyone should participate directly in all aspects of strategic decision-making of relevance to them. The final chapter examines practical and positive ways of proceeding in the context of issues such as privatization, inward investment, new technology, Europe and the regions. However, at a more general level four points warrant particular emphasis.

First, the key feature of a democratic economy is that people take on new roles in society. The idea is to move away from strategic decision-making being the exclusive preserve of an élite. Rather, participation in strategic decision-making will be opened to people more generally, and as a consequence constraints on the development and use of people's talents and abilities will be lifted: participation provides 'good' government but also better individuals (Lively 1975, p. 132). It has been recently argued that the Japanese firm is characterized by a non-hierarchical coordination of production, with employees actively participating in decision-making (Aoki 1990b). However, it is clear that there is nothing in Aoki that would suggest that the strategic oversight of the Japanese firm is determined by any more than a tiny minority of those involved with the firm. Clearly workers have a voice within the Japanese firm; the joint consultation schemes allow discussion of important areas (see Koike 1990). But employee participation in operational decision-making does not deny the more fundamental point that the choice of organization form suits the strategic decision-makers. Likewise current adaptations towards Japanese structures by Western firms are also in line with this conclusion. Thus new roles are being taken, but these are very much circumscribed and shaped by the élite. A democratic economy requires further development of new social roles for people generally within the economy.

Second, we are advocating a planned process, but not central planning. The idea of central planning is in many ways diametrically opposed to the diffused and deconcentrated economy we have in mind. It is certainly diametrically opposed to the form that central planning, or central 'administration' (Wilhelm 1985), actually took in the twentieth century (see, for example, Kornai 1990 and Steinherr 1991 on the overweening state in what was actually existing communism). Nevertheless, we are unambiguously advocating a planned process and undoubtedly some will react against this. As Robert Reich has observed: 'Americans don't like central planning, they don't like complicated plans, and they especially don't trust business-government-and-labour élites to do the planning. These biases are as populist as apple pie, running clear across the political spectrum and rooted deep in our political history' (quoted in Norton 1986).

Perhaps the sentiments expressed above are essentially American, but clearly they have a wider resonance. They are entirely in line with our position. Planning institutions and mechanisms have to be democratic and transparent; they have to build on participation, rather than being imposed from above. Yet it is important to appreciate that all economies are planned; they simply vary as to who plans and how. For instance, there are substantial differences between Japan, Germany, the United States and Britain, yet all have sophisticated planning systems. We shall consider the case of guided market economies like Japan later in this chapter, but one of the central themes of this book has been to look behind the free market façade and examine the nature of the planning system that lies there. A crucial difference between this system and our suggestion of a democratic market economy is that in the former planning is carried out by and in the interests of a far narrower set of people. We advocate a system springing from and planning for the community in general. What appears as entirely reasonable, indeed highly desirable, for the corporation today, that it plans its own future within the economy, should appear in the same light for the broader community.

Third, we are advocating the use of markets. Like the élite in free market systems, communities would use markets to serve their objectives. They can be very effective mechanisms for allocating scarce resources in certain circumstances. They can be a useful tool for interaction and communication between firms, and between firms and consumers. Most importantly, however, markets are only a tool. In a democratic economy they are a tool for communities, as against being a tool for the élite in a free market system. Moreover, markets are one amongst various tools that would be used. This is a clear implication of, for instance, the extensive literature on transactions costs; even if it were feasible, exclusive use of markets is inadvisable because other mechanisms would sometimes enable a particular activity to be carried out more efficiently. The point that markets alone would not enable a community to achieve its objectives is also related to the planning issue. In a free market system, strategic plans are formulated by an élite using non-market mechanisms — for example, by communication, discussion and politicking in meetings of senior managers and board members. So for economies more generally, including democratic economies, the design of plans requires non-market mechanisms; the idea of formulating strategies via a set of markets is not feasible.

Fourth, and finally, the thrust of our analysis points to the need for government, at various levels, to play a vital, constant role in moving the economy towards a more diffuse, less concentrated structure of decision-making: replacing current systems with democratic structures and constantly scrutinizing these new structures for evidence of capture by an élite. We envisage government being involved in both the process of formulating community plans and the derivative process of their implementation. An implication is that policy should be seen in a broad context. Thus policies on privatization, inward investment, technology and monopoly should be both informed and assessed by guiding principles relating to the requirement for democratic decision-making.

One important point of clarification needs to be added at this juncture. Economic democracy is not defined by an economy of autonomous labour-managed firms. Simply replacing the élitist structures of the major corporations with more internally democratic structures is certainly a step in the direction of economic democracy, but it needs to be incorporated in a broader framework. Monopoly control by labour of the supply of specific goods and services can be just as constraining for the development of the rest of the economy as is the present control structure. Economic democracy certainly demands that all the producers of a good or service are represented in strategic decisions relating to its production, but it also requires that the broader community is involved in such strategies. Economic democracy means that the economy is organized and operated in the interests of the whole community and this requires community control of the fundamental decision structure.

A policy framework

We start this section by considering recent experiences in industrial policy-making, both bad and good, before going on to consider a policy framework growing from those experiences but more directly congruent with our guiding principles.

We focus first on two cases of dramatic relative industrial decline over recent history — that of the former Soviet Empire and that of Britain. In the case of actual existing socialism, as it was represented in the traditional Soviet model, its grave inadequacies, whilst being apparent from an early date — indeed, anarchist writers were clear about its fundamental deficiencies in the nineteenth century well before it was put into practice — became increasingly obvious in the

1980s, and culminated with the revolutions of 1989. As indicated in Chapter 1, the decline in production since that date, as these economies have been opened up to open competition with free market economies, has been dramatic. Whilst it can, and should be argued that the opening-up process should have been a more controlled one, this nevertheless does not deny the essential truth that the centrally administered system, with production organized into vertically integrated, industry monopolies, had driven these economies into an economic dead-end. They did not possess the creativity, flexibility or dynamism effectively to cope with the new challenge. They had to be sheltered from it, but this was denied.

The first thing that needs to be said about this major disaster of the twentieth century is that it had nothing to do with anything that can reasonably be represented as socialism; the three major principles of socialism were rejected (Davies 1990). State ownership replaced common ownership, appointed managers replaced democratic management, and equality was seen to be inconsistent with efficiency. It was clear that once state ownership was achieved the principles by which it was allowed to operate were essentially adopted from American capitalism. It is now clear that a bureaucratic, authoritarian and concentrated organization of production, whilst able to engineer a rapid industrialization of an earlier agrarian economy, ultimately ran into fundamental problems in the more complex world of the later twentieth century, whether operating within 'state socialism' or monopoly capitalism. We cannot deny the earlier growth, but it was bought at great cost to the people involved and the environment they lived and worked in and it created a system which has shown an inability to adapt to changes in the world that it created. Our analysis would suggest that it is the lack of democracy characteristic of both systems which has brought the downfall of the one and threatens the downfall of the other.

Britain is another extreme illustration of wrong directions. It is likely that Britain has experienced persistent, unrelieved, relative economic decline since the mid-nineteenth century, but the experience since 1945 has been no less dramatic for that. As Pollard has said, 'this was, after all ... the period when Britain offered the spectacle of the most astonishing relative decline of any economy known to recent history: nothing like it has happened elsewhere in the modern world' (Pollard 1992, p. 1283). Although the recent economic collapse of the Soviet Empire may appear more dramatic, there can be no gainsaying Pollard's observation and thus the need to rethink the overall form and direction of industrial economic policy in Britain.[3] Without denying that specific aspects of policy may have been successful, Britain's poor economic performance and bad experience with particular policy initiatives suggests that, taken as a whole, its industrial policy must be judged unsuccessful. If we start with the ending of the Second World War, we see the rapid discarding of the institutions and mechanisms of planning which had been adopted during the war, and the equally rapid re-emergence of the Treasury as the dominant economics' ministry. Rather than being concerned with the mobilization of the forces of production, policy was again primarily aimed at their containment; inflation and the balance of payments were prior concerns. However, by the early 1960s doubts were creeping in and the Conservative government of the time brought into being a tripartite organization (government, industry and labour) for considering issues of economic policy, the National Economic Development Council. This was subsequently retained by the next, Labour government, and other institutions were quickly added, including a Ministry of Technology and a Department of Economic Affairs, and out of this a national plan was hatched. However, the dominance of the Treasury view had not been effectively challenged; the plan was quickly sacrificed at the altar of short-run macro-policy. Another new institution, the Industrial Reorganization Corporation, lasted a little longer, but it seemed doomed to failure given that it proceeded to invert the fundamental principle on which it had to work: whilst dynamic (private) efficiency may result in large firms, simply creating large, ramshackle empires out of unpromising material is no spur to efficiency; indeed, just the opposite is true.

With the advent of the Labour governments of the 1970s came a whole new raft of policy institutions, but nothing substantial happened. Planning agreements spluttered into life but were quickly extinguished, the National Enterprise Board became a repository for lame ducks, the nationalizations of the period appeared as a largely unwarranted diversion of time and effort and were never used to promote the development of an overall strategy for the economy (Hare 1985). The whole affair revealed a lack of serious commitment to transforming the processes of economic development.

Summing up the experiences of the whole post-war period until the early 1980s, it could reasonably be concluded that there was 'no coherence, consistence or persistence in British policy towards industry' (Sharp and Shepherd 1987). There were plenty of policies towards industry, 'at one time or another, the British have employed virtually every industrial policy tool' (Eads and Yamamura 1987), but either they were *ad hoc* solutions to specific problems, or fashionable cures quickly discarded. Eads and Yamamura conclude that 'almost all of these experiments ... have been judged failures, and not just by those critical of industrial policy in general'. Yet some have pointed to a substantial growth in manufacturing productivity in the 1980s and have argued that the British economy has been demonstrating renewed vigour. These observations might be seen as effectively pointing to an appropriate way forward. However, we would suggest that this improved performance is a one-off which may reverse itself (see Cowling 1990). The fundamental source for 1980s productivity growth in Britain was the substantial rise in the pace of work. Such a rise could not continue for ever. It is of the nature of human endeavour that its intensity cannot be increased without limit; hence we cannot presume that greater work intensity would raise produc- tivity in the future, even if this is thought desirable. Indeed, exactly the reverse could be the case, due to a legacy of resentment following from the initial imposition of greater effort. We suggest that higher rates of productivity growth can only be maintained by a funda- mental change in the way we approach industrial investment, research and development, education and training; these are activi- ties in which Britain's performance has been inferior to that of its major rivals and in which the degree of inferiority has worsened (Crafts 1991).

Thus the fundamentals of the British economy are not right. Its rate of growth in the late 1980s was internationally respectable because of the slackening of fiscal and monetary policy over that period, and the associated substantial depreciation of sterling, but it proved unsus- tainable and the subsequent reining-back of the economy plunged Britain into negative growth. The record of successive Conservative governments since 1979 is not impressive. For the period through to the end of 1992 the growth of Gross Domestic Product averaged only 1.5 per cent p.a., with the inflation rate averaging 6.5 per cent and the unemployment rate about the highest amongst the major industrial countries. Although Britain may experience some short-term improvement from the deep and extended recession of the early 1990s, significant long-term improvement cannot be expected under existing policies because they neglect the real bases of industrial dynamism.

In contrast to Britain and its close ally in policy-making, the United States, some of their international trading rivals have recognized the case for an explicit national and/or regional industrial economic strategy, operating within and around the market system, to help secure the ambitions of national and/or regional communities.[4] Japan, the Four Dragons of the Pacific Rim, and certain regions in Europe, such as Emilia Romagna in Italy and Baden Württemburg in Germany are cases in point, perhaps the most obvious ones. In each case the formulation and implementation of an industrial strategy appears to have been associated with considerable economic success, at least as measured by the rate of growth in output.

The Japanese saw early on that static comparative advantage was not an adequate basis for national economic development; after the Second World War that would have left them as producers of rice, cheap toys and simple textiles. To break out into other areas of economic activity required that the state should be directly involved in the economic system: the market could not be relied on. The market had to be managed and directed — a national economic strategy had to be imposed. Although various departments and agencies of the state are involved in industrial strategy, the Ministry of International Trade and Industry (MITI) has a central and dominant role (see Johnson 1982, which offers a particularly illuminating account of its work). MITI proceeds by targeting certain sectors which appear to have a key role within the economy at a particular stage of its development. These are chosen after wide-ranging consultation and discussion throughout industry. MITI then acts to ensure that, by a variety of interventions, these sectors grow rapidly and efficiently. One key aspect at the time of rapid development in the 1950s and early 1960s was the protection of domestic industry until it was internationally fully competitive; protection was used as an enabling condition for rapid restructuring and development. As a consequence a substantial degree of domestic rivalry evolved in most industries selected for this treatment: rather than attempting to pick winners, Japanese policy seeks to create a stable from which winners will emerge. MITI relies heavily on market forces to support its own measures, and is undoubtedly helped in this by the long-term perspectives of the typical Japanese industrial firm, untrammelled by the threat of an active market for corporate control and supported by the long-term commitment of Japanese financial capital. The keys to success in Japanese planning have been wide consultation, serious effort to reach agreement on the form of intervention, and the avoidance of day-to-day interference in operational decision-making (Hare 1985). Planning has been strategic, but based on some notion of consensus.

We have quite deliberately avoided getting into the detail of policy-making in Japan; its various instruments, institutions and mechanisms are a product of its own history and culture, and it would generally be wrong to consider that they could, or indeed should be transplanted to countries with quite different historical and cultural circumstances: this sort of magpie behaviour is all too common and all too unsuccessful — witness problems with just-in-time production in British industry. What is important to learn from the Japanese case is the approach to the problem. For other countries to be as successful will require the same degree of commitment of government to economic development: the whole Japanese state is organized around the needs of economic development — it is a developmental state (Johnson 1982). But governments' involvement should be strategic, rather than getting involved in operational detail. Its role has to be seen as catalytic, proactive rather than reactive. Policy in most Western countries tends to be *ad hoc* and reactive because of a suspicion of state planning. The message of the Japanese experience is that planning and the market have to be integrated in the process of development.

Japan, then, is the most important case of the government taking on a central developmental role in the economy without, in recent history, directly owning or controlling most of the productive assets. Discussions of planning or the market typically confuse two distinct dichotomies, state intervention versus *laissez-faire* and market versus non-market forms of organization (Neuburger 1985). To avoid this confusion we have to separate planning from the question of nationalization and this Japan successfully does. The success of the Japanese economy since 1945 is obvious (see Chapter 1): they were able to establish a remarkable dynamism over an extended period which we believe has not been extinguished despite the present financial crisis. But the question arises as to what extent the Japanese success story relates to government industrial strategy. A debate on this question has raged since the early 1970s without reaching any clear-cut solution. This is not surprising since mainstream economics offers only limited accommodation to ideas of industrial strategy-making. The major advocates of moves in this direction tend to come from outside mainstream economics: from political science (for instance, Johnson 1982; Reich 1983, 1991), from sociology (Dore 1986), from business schools (Porter 1990), from political circles (for example, Heseltine 1987 and the Labour Party 1993), as well, of course, from more heterodox positions within the economics profession (for example, Best 1990; Cowling and Sugden 1990; and Sharp 1993). It is such people who have looked at government's role in Japan and come to the view that it has been both important and a basis for learning about a different way forward for other countries, almost despite the prevailing orthodoxy in economics. But the orthodoxy has not remained unchanged; a limited but clearly apparent adjustment in positions is taking place (see, for example, Krugman 1987 and Dornbusch *et al.* 1989).

Whilst Japan can be seen as the most important case of industrial strategy-making within a market economy, the recent history of the Four Dragons of the Pacific Rim is both interesting and illuminating, and, as we saw in Chapter 1, it relates to a pattern of phenomenal economic success. For a considerable period the experiences of Singapore, Hong Kong, Taiwan and South Korea were taken as strong evidence in favour of the innate dynamism of free market economies (see, for example, in the case of Taiwan, Little 1979 and Ranis 1979) — the rest of the undeveloped world could only hope to develop by opening up their own economies to the forces of the free market as the Dragons had obviously done. Then people started examining these rapidly developing economies a little more closely. It became apparent that they could not adequately be described as free market economies — government was taking on an active, variable, but quite central role within the development of the industrial economy (Lim 1983; White 1988; Amsden 1989; Wade 1990; Westphal 1990). Again there seems to have been confusion in discussions of planning or the market — as with Japan the Four Dragons offer dramatic illustrations of the potential significance of a strategic role for government within industry without wholesale nationalization, although the extent of the public ownership of productive assets varies substantially among the Four Dragons, with Taiwan relying extensively on public enterprise and Hong Kong very little. In fact, as was suggested in Chapter 1, Hong Kong is probably the weakest example of industrial strategy-making by government within the group of four and there is some evidence that it has suffered as a result in terms of a rather limited restructuring of its export base compared with the other three, a weakness that was recognized in the 1987 proposals by the Hong Kong government on 'radical departure' (Wade 1990).[5]

Because of their dramatic success the East Asian cases we have reported are important in arguing the case for industrial strategy. They are useful in helping undermine the myth of the unique efficiency of the free market. However, this does not mean that lessons from their experience are easily drawn. It is clear that these various cases do *not* fit our idea of a democratic market economy — they represent only a step away from a free market economy. Neither can we assume that industrial strategy-making of the present East Asian variety will be equally successful elsewhere, given the experiences of many unsuccessful government interventions within Europe, Latin America and Africa (Westphal 1990). Nevertheless, the successes of Japan and the Four Dragons does reveal that with the right approach a competent government can intervene in ways which appear consistent with a remarkable economic dynamism. Examples of such success are also available in Europe, but they appear most evident at regional rather than national level, which may point to the requirement for a strong sense of identity in order to achieve success, perhaps an important lesson in itself when prospecting for a way forward.[6] The Third Italy, that region between the older industrialized areas of the North and the primarily agricultural South beginning in and around Emilia-Romagna and extending out to neighbouring areas, seems to have attracted most attention (see, for example, Brusco 1982; Piore and Sabel 1984; Best 1990; and Dei Ottati 1991). A dynamic regional economy appears to have been created with the emergence of a network of technologically sophisticated, highly flexible, small-scale manufacturing firms creating Marshall's idea of an industrial district. The emergence of such a modern and successful network appears to have been significantly influenced by the supportive industrial strategy of the regional government providing conditions in which small firms, via a process of collective entrepreneurialism (Best 1990), could escape their earlier dependence on large firms, typically from outside the region, and establish independent access to the (international) market. Baden Württemberg is another European example of successful, active, regional industrial strategy (see Löhn and Stadelmeier 1990), and there are many more.

At this point we would simply wish to conclude that in approaching the question of industrial economic policy in the context of existing free market economies, there are a number of examples scattered around the world where government at national or regional level may have had an essentially positive impact on the processes of industrial development. No doubt some will view the examples described as cases of catch-up within a perfectly natural market process, rather than having anything to do with purposive government intervention within that process. However, as we maintained in Chapter 1, there is nothing in the catch-up hypothesis to explain changes in the rankings among followers as has occurred, particularly the relative success of our examples of systemic industrial strategy-making (Gordon 1992). This is not to deny the existence of government failure in perhaps many cases; rather it is to suggest that there is evidence around, for those willing to look, to suggest that the careful development of policy in this area warrants as serious attention as does the development of other areas of economic policy-making. This involves learning from the successful and unsuccessful examples which are available.

At the same time it is obvious that none of these economies with well-developed and apparently successful industrial strategies fully conforms to the guiding principles we have suggested.[7] This is one reason why we would not wish to advocate that a particular locality should slavishly follow the details of any of their examples — the other reason being, as we mentioned in the Japanese case, that circumstances differ, as a matter of history and everything that derives from that: culture, society, polity and economy. However, by having an industrial strategy where government is accountable in some way to a democratic policy, these countries have moved at least part way towards democratizing strategic decision-making within the economy. In this context, Ozaki (1984) has argued that the Western economic paradigm, based on ownership of productive assets, is inadequate in classifying the Japanese economic system, where, as we have previously argued, although the public sector is small, intervention is large. He sees the Japanese economy as capitalist, but he does not see it as a free market economy. He goes on to argue that there is a gap in economic policy-making in the West, with the focus being almost exclusively on short-run macroeconomic policy without any complementary long-run policy providing perspective and direction. In contrast, in Japan, industrial strategy transcends this scenario; it provides the link between the short- and long-term aspects of policy-making.

The other sense in which the Japanese case represents a move in the direction of a democratic economy is in terms of the nature of the Japanese firm. Whilst we would not accept Aoki's (1990b) view that it is under the dual control of workers and finance, we would accept that its internal structure is much more conducive to an outcome which reflects a broader array of interests than is the case for Western corporations — Koike (1990) records how most Japanese establishments have joint consultation schemes covering important areas of operational policy-making. This accords with Odagiri's (1992) observations as to the growth-maximizing behaviour of Japanese management, and its preference for internal growth over mergers and acquisitions. Internal growth is sought because Japanese firms recognize that their human resources are the firm's most important asset and organize the firm accordingly. People see their futures linked to the organization and are therefore concerned with the future of the firm and their place within it, and internal growth creates a widening span of opportunities for both managers and other employees. But the pursuit of growth puts the firm in conflict with rivals — it is a stimulus to a variety of forms of long-run competition. The consequence is a highly dynamic economy, but one which is stable over the cycle because of the internal pressures within the firm to maintain employment in recession. This characteristic of the Japanese economy is being severely tested at the present time.

Our general principles, coupled with the sort of observations made above about Japan, would suggest the need for a dual-track approach, involving both changing the environment within which enterprises make strategic decisions and changing the nature of firms themselves. This would imply a recognition that the institutions of the free market economy are characterized by socially incomplete decision structures and the remedy requires both the entry of new actors, representing the community as a whole, into market processes and structural, and therefore behavioural, changes in the individual strategic decision-making units. Policy will therefore have two basic dimensions: the first viewing corporate structures as parametric with policy instruments seeking changes in strategic decisions via a public strategy on industries and sectors; the second viewing corporate structures as variables to be influenced in appropriate ways, for example, by changes in company law and corporate tax policies, aimed at securing a broader representation of interests within the firm (see Knight and Sugden 1990), and the encouragement of small-scale enterprise structures.

The problem of agency

In proposing remedies for the inadequacies of free market economies we have advanced the notion of community control over strategic decisions within the economy. To many this will appear as a replacement of an economic concentration of power with an even more overweening concentration of political power over the economy, with national government, or even supranational government (as with Brussels) establishing an even greater grip over the affairs of the region or nation. If this were the outcome then our whole purpose would have been undermined. We have sought to establish the view that social efficiency in the absence of democracy is a chimera: the one cannot be achieved without the other. But if the state is to usurp the wishes of the people, then there can be no presumption that replacing the power of corporate élites with political élites will increase welfare; indeed, the experience of the Soviet Union and Central and Eastern Europe would suggest that, within the economy at least, the change could well be for the worse.

This is a serious matter. The advocacy of a strategic role for government within the market economy has to recognize the inevitable problems of agency that will be raised and has to point to the necessity of designing institutions capable of making economic democracy a reality rather than a charade. In calling for community control we are not simply calling for control over the corporate economy, but also for control over the institutions of the state: transparency and accountability in the workings of government are not optional extras but absolute necessities. Thus we are explicitly attempting not to repeat the lack of logical reciprocity that appears to characterize mainstream arguments against the involvement of government in the market. Just as the relevance of the role of the market is not denied by the mainstream, despite the incidence of market failure, so the relevance of the role of government should not be denied as an actor within the market economy, despite the existence of government failure. Just as the possibility of market failure demands a regulatory role for the state, for example, in terms of traditional monopolies and merger policy, so we should design governmental structures with the transparency and accountability to ensure their adequate regulation by the community at large. Our ultimate aim must be a community's government.

Thus we have established some general principles, but the way these are built upon is all-important. Learning from past mistakes and successful experiences matters, but more is needed. As discussed earlier, the record of the state takeover of industry in the Soviet Union and the attempts at industrial intervention in Britain offer examples where government involvement in industrial development has in general not been a happy one, to say the least. A successful industrial strategy requires competence and commitment, and this is the lesson we must learn from the experience of countries like Japan. But we must also be clear that we do not advocate copying Japan — the Japanese system is far away from our objective of a democratic market economy. It vital to take positive steps to avoid excessive concentration of political power in the economy. For instance, whilst industrial strategy-making within Europe at both national and Europe-wide levels is a crucial part of the whole, given that the most powerful private economic organizations, the major corporations, will otherwise exist outside democratic control, nevertheless the re-creation of meaningful local and regional economies via the actions of local and regional community institutions must underpin the work of government at national and European level (for an interesting discussion, see Sabel 1988). Such bottom-up structures will help ensure the avoidance of the growth of the concentration of political power arising from the extension of economic policy-making into the market. Whilst the slackening of control by government at the centre is not easily achievable it is something that has to be actively worked for if we are ever to see an effective economic democracy. Within Europe, perhaps paradoxically, the structures of the institutions of the European Union appear to offer a route by which regions within existing European nations may achieve a greater degree of autonomy. We shall investigate this matter further in the final chapter.

Notes

1   Earlier versions of parts of this analysis are reported in Cowling and Sugden (1993a, 1993b).
2   Our focus on the Anglo-American version is not a matter of parochialism; with some significant exceptions, such structures have inspired widespread imitation in the twentieth century.
3   Pollard himself has put the blame fairly and squarely on the Treasury's shoulders, which he describes as having a 'contempt for production' (Pollard 1982).
4   Some might be inclined to put the countries of the former Soviet Empire in the same category as the United States and Britain, given their record since 1989 in seeking free market solutions to their problems. However, whilst it is probably true that powerful factions within these countries were inclined to favour free market ideology, the decisive influence would appear to have been the International Monetary Fund's explicit denial of industrial strategy as an acceptable economic policy within its conditions of approval for funding arrangements.
5   Of course, the growing uncertainty and apprehension about the future of Hong Kong has inevitably played a major part in Hong Kong's economic development in recent years. Nevertheless, the possibility of enormous benefits of a closer attachment to China also remains.
6   It is notable that the Four Dragons are all small countries, and while Japan is much larger, it is a country which is culturally quite homogeneous with a strong sense of national identity and purpose. In comparison nation states within Europe appear much more fragmented.
7   However, many aspects of policy-making in the Third Italy fit in very nicely within our guiding principles — for example, the emphasis on community-based policy-making aimed at sustaining small-scale enterprises within active local networks of firms. We shall return to this focus later.

7

BUILDING A NEW ECONOMY: TOPICAL ISSUES

Having established a solid foundation for building a new economy by developing a set of guiding principles, we now turn to some topical and pressing issues and address them within a framework provided by those principles. The issues covered are privatization, particularly in the context of Central and Eastern Europe and the former Soviet Union; inward investment and technology policy within a European, but also more general context; and finally Europe and the regional dimension, specifically within the context of the European Union, but again with much more general implications. Whilst these issues have a substantial resonance within the Third World, we do not devote space to developing a detailed appreciation of that context; we limit ourselves to identifying a need for a complete reappraisal of IMF/World Bank policy towards both the Third World and the former centrally administered economies. A more considered treatment of the Third World, though obviously important, is beyond our present capacity and must remain as an unfulfilled ambition.

We must emphasize again that, unlike the traditional approach to industrial economic policy, the basis for our analysis of these issues is not one which starts with markets and the consideration of market failure. Our policy perspective recognizes that markets have a role as an important instrument of economic development, but only as an instrument. We have chosen to root our analysis in the socially incomplete nature of strategic decision-making in modern corporations. We have identified the strategic planning of industrial activity as the key issue for industrial development and thus advocate strategic planning by communities as the core issue for industrial policy. These two issues do not feature in the market failure approach. We do not seek to deny that traditional policy areas, such as monopoly and merger, remain important and indeed crucial in building a democratic market economy. However, they need to be set alongside a wider set of concerns, simultaneously addressed as part of a coherent approach to policy design and, most importantly, addressed from a strategy-making perspective. The fundamental problem with the market failure approach is that it does not and cannot offer this perspective.

The privatization issue[1]

Privatization may have started within Thatcherism in Britain but it has become the current vogue across much of the world economy. Throughout much of Europe and the Third World it is taken as a panacea for a multitude of ills — it has a clear political resonance in a world plagued by large and mounting public sector deficits. But it is within the former centrally administered economies of Central and Eastern Europe and the Soviet Union, with their essentially state-owned production sector, where the issue of privatization looms largest. Privatization now has a clear centrality within the restructuring of these economies, implying a sharp discontinuity with previous reforms. Over the previous thirty years or so reform concentrated on decentralization and marketization — ownership was not seen as one of the central issues — but, as Gomulka (1991) puts it, the present reform is 'no longer the marketisation of Soviet socialism but the embracement of Western (welfare state) capitalism'.

Whilst many people appear to see privatization in a largely unproblematic light, it has recently been suggested that there is no formal theoretical case within mainstream economics for privatization (see, for example, Grosfeld 1990).[2] For some this is an argument against blanket solutions, but others, for example Grosfeld, seem undeterred and argue that efficiency will be stimulated because shareholders have stronger incentives to pressure managers. But it is not clear why this should be so. There will always be a problem of asymmetric information between principal and agent. It would seem that the form or nature of the relationship between principal and agent is the essence of the problem, rather than whether the principal is public or private. Notice how performance within the public sector varies from polity to polity: within nations, witness the Third Italy (for example, Emilia

Romagna) versus the Second (Mezzogiorno); between nations, witness the evidence on the dynamism of public enterprise in China, given recent reforms (Nolan 1991), compared with the failure of similar reforms within the Soviet Empire; and indeed, over time, witness the significant improvements observed in Britain prior to privatization, revealing how the pressure on management by public principals to improve performance was effective — indeed, some have argued that essentially all the observed improvement in privatized enterprises came about prior to privatization!

However, the argument for privatization can be extended: if control of managers by owners fails, and adequate incentives cannot be designed, then takeover can reassert the interests of shareholders. In other words, the market for corporate control will re-establish efficiency. But this argument is also of dubious validity; all the evidence points to the inefficiency-promoting activities of the market for corporate control (see, for example, Scherer and Ross 1990), and also its existence is likely to impose a short-termist perspective on decision-making (see the discussion in Chapter 3). Nevertheless, the advocates of privatization persist: 'all imperfections of capital market and market for corporate control notwithstanding, they still seem the key elements of the market environment which East Europeans are looking for' (Grosfeld 1990). Let us consider this, step by step.

The *raison d'être* for privatization requires the creation of an 'owning group' with sufficient power to challenge the prerogatives of management; otherwise efficiency could be achieved by the decentralization of decision-making within the state sector without too much concern with questions of ownership. (Clearly, there would be real political issues to be resolved, but so there are in entrusting the state with the process of privatization.) Thus two breaks are seen to be required: the break from central administration and control, and also the break from managerial control. Note that the argument for privatization cannot be a matter of managerial incentives because decentralization/marketization (if into a competitive market) should establish the incentives (see Nolan 1991 for the China case), and privatization in itself does not ensure that managerial incentives are established — for example, the tax system could discourage enterprise.

There appear to be two routes for achieving a concentration of 'ownership' sufficient effectively to challenge the prerogatives of management. The first route could be termed the big capital solution, which can be achieved directly by selling off to big capital, which in many cases will mean foreign capital, or, indirectly, via a wide-scale distribution of shares to inexpert owners, followed by the almost inevitable concentration of ownership in that group with relative wealth and power. In post-communist societies such a group will significantly intersect with the former nomenklatura — indeed, this may seem by those seeking it to be one of the cheapest and least problematic routes for the establishment of big capital in these economies, given that so-called spontaneous privatization (the takeover of state assets by the former nomenklatura) may be seen to lack legitimacy.

The second route would be a democratic solution and three examples are offered. First is the broadening of the membership of the joint stock company to include employees, suppliers, the community, as discussed in Chapter 6. One consequence of this would be that the principal–agent problems arising from an information asymmetry would be reduced because of greater internal or connected representation within the firm, in contrast to the external or disconnected representation of most shareholders with the joint stock company. The concentration of 'ownership', or, strictly speaking, membership, can then be achieved via institutions such as trusts, with collective power invested in trustees (see Knight and Sugden 1990). Our second example, self-management, implying the transfer of ownership to a collective of workers/producers (including management), who would then be able to elect, control and remove managers, obviously offers a more democratic solution than the capitalist firm, but, as we have previously argued, it stops short of community control. Finally, a third example would be a new transparent and accountable public ownership, one requiring election to boards and democratic supervision of management. This would imply the transformation of the notion of public ownership from the model embedded in present and former nationalized industries to something that might be more accurately called common ownership, the original aim of those advocating socialism in the nineteenth century.

From what we have said throughout this book our preference for the democratic solution over the big capital solution is clear. One way of expressing this would be to say that we seek power as a *countervailing* power, rather than as a *successive* power. If we were to control managerial prerogatives by substituting the prerogatives of another élite group, it is not clear that progress would be made. A first best solution requires control over management without the concentration of private power, that is, a democratic solution. Thus the objective would be to establish, within or without the privatisation process, democratic control over private accretions of power. And, as argued earlier, policy would also be directed at creating diffuse and deconcentrated structures where accretions of power will inevitably be kept to a minimum.

It is clear that the present conjuncture in Central and Eastern Europe and the former Soviet Union presents both a significant opportunity and serious dangers. The lack of balanced and efficient economic development, the creation of inefficient and unwieldy monocultures instead of integrated, diversified and adaptive economic regions and communities, represent a tragedy of Europe's post-Second World War history, a tragedy that will take a lot of time to reverse.[3] But one dogma has replaced another; as Kowalik (1991) has said, 'The authorities regard privatisation as the ultimate purpose of the systemic changes'. Our analysis points to the requirement for an opening-up of existing structures in order to establish community control. Privatization may be consistent with this in that it can provide an opportunity for fracturing the link with an élitist system of control. This becomes the central reason for privatization, the reason why it can be seen as progressive by a wide range of political opinion. But the basic need is for economic democracy, and privatization provides one potential instrument for achieving this, but one among many, and one whose effectiveness towards this end is by no means unconditional and unambiguous. What is desperately needed is the time and space for nations and communities more generally to begin to conduct their own experiments. Even those extolling the virtues of mass privatization seem dubious about the spontaneous, nomenklatura privatizations which have loomed large in some countries: 'laissez-faire is not the right policy to re-establish laissez-faire', says Wellicz (1991). But the reason why it should be seen as unsatisfactory is because of the uneven balance of power which gets in the way of an efficient and equitable outcome. Blanchard and Layard (1991) are wrong to see this simply as a matter of fairness: spontaneous privatization offers a convenient way of moving from one inefficient, élitist system to another. In order to avoid such a transformation from 'state socialism' to monopoly capitalism, great care needs to be exercised with privatization and more generally with the structure of control — it needs incorporating into a more broadly based industrial strategy which seeks to begin the process of transformation of centrally administered economies into democratic market economies rather than free market economies as we see them at the end of the twentieth century. This means a planned process: one in which the big monopolies are, wherever possible, broken down into meaningful smaller enterprises; where experimentation is allowed with the type of organization; and finally where meaningful regional economies and communities are created. Structures appropriate to the evolution of a more democratic economy can be created most readily in the *ex-ante* planning of the privatization process, rather than within the *ex-post* regulation of its unplanned outcomes. Without this, Lombardini's (1992) prediction that '... privatisation may provide the historical opportunity for a class of a few, very rich people to emerge in the USSR' may turn out to be an accurate one.

The pursuit of inward investment

The question of inward investment has become a central issue within the context of the policies of many national governments over recent years, but particularly those espousing the virtues of the market, like the British Conservative governments of the 1980s and early 1990s and those governments of Central and Eastern Europe and the former Soviet Union which have been recently seduced or impelled by such arguments, together with others who have been pushed into opening themselves up to inward investment as a consequence of the conditionality attached to IMF/World Bank financial backing. Whatever the underlying impetus, the international pursuit of inward investment has intensified markedly and remains firmly at or near the top of the policy agenda for the foreseeable future. Within Britain, it underpins the current concern with the Social Chapter provisions of the Maastricht Treaty and the proposal to restrict working hours to forty-eight within the Union. The British government is attempting to promote Britain as a low labour-cost economy within Western Europe to achieve inward investment (see also Chapter 4). Thus Britain is acting in a way which rekindles the arguments made by those who feared social dumping as a likely consequence of the creation of the Single Market, the notable element being that this card is being played by a country whose wage costs, although much lower than some in the Union, are certainly nowhere near the bottom of the league table.

The first thing we might say about inward investment is that it has certain affinities with privatization as an element of policy-making and it is therefore not surprising that governmental preference for the one will tend to be associated with preference for the other. In both cases, rather than seeking to resolve the perceived inadequacies of the sector in question within that sector, whether public or private, the problems are simply hived off. It reflects a particular way of viewing the organization of production and the working of the market economy; it denies the ability of production units to reform themselves, given appropriate incentives to do so, instead relying either on the spontaneous creation of allegedly superior organizations, as a result of a change in ownership, or on existing, outside (foreign) organizations, which are in some unspecified way allegedly efficient. Policy, in this sense, does not entail an enquiry into organization and efficiency, but merely the replacement of one allegedly less efficient organization by another, whether it be private enterprise replacing public, or foreign enterprise replacing indigenous. The attention is on the market rather than the organization; policy is directed at opening up more of the economy to the full thrust of market forces, rather than aimed at improving the functioning of indigenous organizations, whether public or private. This has been one of the singular features of the management of the British economy, which positions it as an extreme case of a free market economy — even the United States, which is often taken to be the free market economy par excellence, seems much more sensitive to the possible deleterious effects of inward investment (see Bailey *et al*. 1994).[4]

When judging the appropriateness of inward investment to the objective of raising the level of economic performance of a particular country, we have first to recognize the simple fact that the strategic decisions resulting in that investment are being taken in the corporate interest, consonant with the objectives of an elite which may have little commitment to the country or locality in question. There is no reason why this should be congruent with the democratic interest in that country. This does not rule out inward investment: what it means is that inward investment has to be positioned within a broader strategy within which it does contribute to that democratic interest. A socially complete decision structure has to be imposed, but this should be seen as a positive rather than negative policy, seeking ways in which the strategy of the inward investor can be adapted to the needs of the community. We have argued earlier that this broader strategy is likely to be consistent with the development of a durable dynamism of national, regional and local economy, and inward investment can play a role. Whilst many countries do attach conditions to inward investment, many small, low-income economies find it difficult to do so and some essentially choose not to do so. The approach of successive British governments, whether Conservative or Labour, puts them in the latter group — a largely unqualified acceptance of the case for inward investment (see Sugden 1989). There has been little monitoring of its actual consequences for Britain, and yet it would seem clear that the belief in its alleged benefits, in terms of balance of payments, employment and technology base, is not built on particularly secure foundations. Whilst temporary gains in these areas may be observed, a long-term commitment to specific locations cannot be assured, and even where an investment of longer-term duration is made, it cannot be assumed that such activity is congruent with the national interest. Research and development would be a case in point. Whilst the establishment of such facilities in, say, Britain by foreign-based transnationals is often seen to be particularly beneficial, it is not clear that embedding British scientific and engineering expertise into the corporate structures of such firms represents the best use of indigenous talent. There is an alternative: indigenous talent can be harnessed to indigenous enterprise to create a locally based and more durable dynamism within the community. But that will require a strategy which shapes the market in the interest of the community, rather than the present policies which shape communities in the interest of the market.

Whilst evidence may be scarce in the United Kingdom, Ireland, following a similar policy of unqualified enthusiasm for inward investment, has recorded a wealth of experience relating to the impact of inward investment in the absence of an overall industrial strategy. It appears that the three phases of inward investment in Ireland '... led to increased output and employment for a time, but none as yet has created the basis for lasting expansion' (Kennedy *et al.*, 1992). The same authors conclude, 'the Irish branches were often little more than production platforms which had few linkages with the rest of the economy. They did not therefore go far towards building an indigenous innovative capacity that would be more likely to endure'. Scottish experience reveals a similar lack of connection with the local economy by foreign transnationals (Turok 1993). A survey of the electronics industry reveals that the plants set up as a result of inward investment bought only 12 per cent of their components and material inputs from Scottish-based companies.

Despite this rather unpromising experience recorded in Ireland and Scotland, there has been a further, recent attempt to justify the promotion of inward investment by people now centrally involved in government policy-making in Britain (see Eltis and Fraser 1992). Their article documents the Japanese transformation of the United Kingdom colour television and motor car industries and argues that such a transformation was necessary to achieve present levels of performance. In the case of colour television this has left Japanese firms in sole control, as happened earlier with motorcycles, and in the case of motor vehicles the remaining large domestic assembler (Rover Group) has just been taken over by a German assembler (BMW). The issue that arises is whether this is a satisfactory outcome as far as British industrial policy and performance is concerned. Superficially there is an appealing logic to the Eltis and Fraser position, but on closer inspection it is revealed to be fundamentally flawed. In both industries earlier policies of protection and subsidy and, in the case of the car industry, the creation of a national champion (British Leyland), did not work. It was also clear for both industries that Japanese producers had achieved a position of world leadership. What could be more logical than to put these two facts together and come up with a welcoming policy for Japanese inward investment? However, is it not ironic that it is to Japan that Britain has turned to secure the benefits of what Eltis and Fraser refer to as 'open competition', that is, the market solution they seek, when these Japanese industries were created as a matter of purposive government strategy within Japan, a purposive strategy which specifically contained 'open competition' to domestic competition over its formative stages? Thus, Japanese strategy included a period of protection, but two other conditions necessary for achieving a successful outcome were also met. The activities protected were, in the long term, appropriate for the Japanese economy, and policies were in place to secure this potential. Such policies were represented in an appropriately articulated industrial strategy, proactive and creative, capable of cementing the long-term ambitions of firms and government. This was the missing element in Britain: protection was tried, but it was never embedded in an industrial strategy aimed at transforming industrial fundamentals — there was little that was proactive and creative in the relationship between government and industry. Again is it not ironic that in reflecting on the success of Japanese-managed plants in foreign locations Eltis and Fraser are also undermining the view that we cannot learn from Japan about running industry because their culture is so different. If culture matters then it would appear that it can be created as a matter of policy, and if it can be created as a matter of policy at the British work-place, why not at the level of government?

In contrast to the British position of unqualified enthusiasm, it is instructive to observe how the Japanese approach to inward investment has evolved over time (see, for example, Bailey *et al.* 1994). In the earlier post-war period both inward and outward investment was tightly controlled. Over the past thirty years there has been a graded liberalization in response to international pressures, but throughout there has been an explicit awareness of the potential problems involved, and barriers have been lowered only when it was felt that the industry in question was strong enough to compete with foreign investment. More recently policy on inward investment has taken on a more positive dimension; in certain key industries policy has been aimed at bringing in foreign transnationals with certain technological expertise and linking them into domestic technology complexes. This would seem a particularly important lesson to learn from Japan. Rather than *laissez-faire*, inward investment needs positioning within the matrix of intra-sectoral relationships so that the potential wider benefits of entry into the domestic economy can be realized. At the best of times the market finds it difficult to handle the innovation and diffusion of new technology, and where the source of that technology is a new foreign entrant there is an even more compelling case for government being an active partner in facilitating this process. We have already noticed the limited impact of inward investment in Scotland and Ireland because of its limited connection with the local economy in which it finds itself. For countries in the Third World with a more limited infrastructure the connections are likely to be even more tenuous — all the more reason why policy should seek to expand and develop these connections rather than simply welcoming inward investment then leaving it as an isolated platform of production adding nothing to the underlying vitality of the economy.

Technology policy

As alluded to in the last section, there is a wide acceptance of the case for government involvement in the development of technology, given the many and obvious reasons for market failure in this area of economic activity, with appropriability being a central one (see, for example, Stoneman and Vickers 1988; House of Lords 1988). Simply the market does not offer the appropriate incentives for the generation and diffusion of new knowledge because of the nature of information itself. It is difficult to evaluate information without knowing what it is, but if you know what it is there is no longer the need to buy it and a regulatory response (for example, patents) simply gets in the way of the diffusion of new knowledge, which, once discovered, should optimally be freely available to all. Whilst it is possible to demonstrate that the market will yield too much research and development — for example, firms may get locked into a socially unproductive product rivalry involving minimal product differentiation but substantial industry-wide investment — nevertheless the usual presumption is that, left to its own devices, too little will be done so that government needs to step in to raise the level beyond that which the market would choose to deliver. In contrast to this conventional view that, essentially, the market should remain as the final arbiter of the direction of investment in new technology, with government simply raising the overall momentum by favouring research and development with a variety of stimulatory policies, we would put the policy emphasis much more on the qualitative dimension. Whether the total magnitude of research and development should be raised or not within a particular area of economic activity would be derivative of our overall industrial strategy. The socially incomplete nature of the decision structure within the free market economy means that the pattern of research and development cannot be expected to be socially optimal.

Thus our view on this is that since the development of new technology is so fundamental to the pace, direction and form of industrial development it is necessary to consider the question of government involvement within a much broader perspective. Otherwise it is all too easy for the technology policy of government to become transmuted into simply subsidizing corporate decisions concerning research and development expenditures rather than aiming to raise the basic dynamism of the industrial economy. We would argue that it is necessary to design future government initiatives as part of a wider concern to develop a diffuse, deconcentrated economy consistent with a move away from a concentrated structure of decision-making. Thus in the area of technological change we need to be circumspect about a policy favouring scale. This would suggest that automatic grants and tax incentives are inappropriate because, as Geroski (1990) argues, such subsidies tend disproportionately to benefit large firms because they formally account for most measured research and development expenditure, whereas much activity which could be accurately termed research and development goes unrecorded in smaller organizations. Our analysis suggests that it is inappropriate to favour national champions, which has typified procurement policies throughout Europe (see again Geroski 1990).

This focus away from large organizations may well have a positive impact on innovation, crucially the output of the research and development process. Pavitt et al. (1987) in their research on British firms found that the largest (at least 10,000 employees), whilst accounting for 80 per cent of recorded research and development in 1975, only managed to generate 47 per cent of significant innovations over the period 1970–9. This result finds substantial resonance in recent surveys of innovation research; for example, Scherer and Ross (1990) conclude, '... very high concentration has a positive effect only in rare cases, and more often it is apt to retard progress by restricting the number of independent sources of initiative and by dampening firms' incentive to gain market position through accelerated R&D'. This concurs with the view that the hierarchical large firm is, by its very nature, an essentially stifling organization where individual talent is all too often constrained by institutional strait-jackets. IBM's current dramatic difficulties, despite its former enormous economic power, may be illustrative of the general problem. More generally, it seems likely that promoting an economy of smaller firms will free more and more individuals to pursue their own and their firm's development, and thus encourage innovative activity. Smaller firms can operate in ways that encourage individuals to contribute ideas about development. They can also operate in ways that better facilitate human development, again feeding the innovative process.

Thus a successful system for encouraging technological progress requires far more than the mere absence of large hierarchical firms; especially important is the design of mutually supportive organizations and arrangements to meet the collective needs of smaller firms, that is, public investment in a wider infrastructure rather than state aid in the traditional sense. These needs may focus on, for instance, the availability of sophisticated techniques for designing new products, and access to long-run finance and hands-on managerial advice, identified by Geroski (1990) as important for supporting risky research and development projects (see also Minns and Rogers 1990). To meet these needs the design work need not start from scratch. The Third Italy offers relevant experience of the successful design of supportive structures. Consider the case of CITER (Centro Informazione Tessile dell'Emilia Romagna), a textile and clothing industry support centre for the region (see Best 1990). Created in 1980, it is controlled by 500 member companies via an annually elected Board of Directors, comprising representatives of companies, regional and local government and productive associations. CITER's function is to provide support services for firms in, amongst many other things, technology. One of its activities has been to develop a computer-aided design system, with members either buying the system or paying for the use of the system at CITER.

For our purposes the significant aspect of this initiative is that it appears to be a successful example of a non-hierarchical, cooperative institution supporting small producers by efficiently providing ser-

vices that they collectively require.[5] There are economies of scale associated with the development and use of new techniques and CITER
appears to have obtained such scale economies without the need for
large, hierarchical organizations. Small producers using the computer-aided design system have access to the sort of techniques usually associated with large-scale production, yet they apparently
maintain their independence, including their independence in design
capability. This is precisely the sort of initiative that our theoretical
analysis suggests is essential to successful economic development.

When advocating a diffuse and deconcentrated economy it is natural to look at the Third Italy where the small firms sector has
received so much attention by policy-makers and has been so successful, but lessons can also be drawn from other countries. For
instance, there are interesting cases of industrial districts within the
United States where high-technology industries have developed in
close association with local universities (see Piore and Sabel 1984). The
United States also provides a fascinating history of yeoman democracy
in which the federal government has provided what Piore and Sabel
describe as an indispensable infrastructure of innovation within agriculture. Other similar examples are: the Baden-Württemburg model
of technology transfer (Löhn and Stadelmeier 1990); the collective
procurement arrangements of small firms represented within the
Japanese Electronic Computer company (Anchordoghy 1988); and the
provision of forty-five technical training centres in West Jutland,
Denmark, which appears to have stimulated the dramatic development of a highly diffused engineering industry within an essentially
rural community (Kristensen 1990). All represent successful, varie-
gated examples of the non-hierarchical provision of technology to
systems of small and medium-sized enterprises. Furthermore, where
current technologies necessitate large-scale production, policy should
include efforts to find ways of changing these technologies, having in
mind the initial bias in the process by which these technologies are
selected, on the basis of control as well as efficiency. There can be no
assumption that existing technological structures are either optimal or
invariant.

Thus our approach to technology policy again implies the need to
view government initiatives in a broad context: initiatives to foster
and stimulate technological change should be designed as part of a
wider concern with developing a democratic economy. It is also
important to take account of the various different starting points
facing regions and countries, not least in the contrast between the
established capitalist economies of the West and the once centrally

administered economies. Building diffuse, deconcentrated economies from this contrasting patchwork implies the need for a bottom-up and varied approach rooted in local communities, with these communities encouraged to pursue their common interests at national and pan-European levels. Thus we visualize a European system for stimulating technological progress that builds from local communities, to national communities and thence to a European community. What would be observed at the local level would be a multiplicity of systems each designed to suit local interests, to build upon local history and to feed from local culture. As Sweeney (1992b) maintains, 'it is not surprising ... to find that the dynamic regions of Europe are ones which not only have a strong and pervasive vocational training system but also have a distinctive traditional culture ...' The end result, we suggest, would be a set of inter-linked, dynamic smaller firm economies, within Europe, but potentially within the other major divisions of the world economy as well.

Europe and the regional dimension

This is an appropriate point to consider the specific institutional structures within Europe in order to evaluate how much progress might be made towards the European economy we seek within such existing structures. Many people appear to believe that industrial policy-making in member states of the European Union, which may in the not too distant future incorporate most European states, is now a thing of the past: as nation states our room for manœuvre is very much circumscribed by Brussels. At one level this is increasingly true. The Commission has been seriously concerned with the levels of state aid to industry; witness the numerous disputes with the Italian government where state aid to manufacturing was being provided at three or four times the level reached in the rest of the community (see Commission 1989; Bianchi 1992b). Community policy actively seeks '... to avoid ... monopolisation, excessive concentration and unfair public aids to national companies' (Commission 1990). The Commission argues that firms are being compensated for inefficiency rather than helped to remove its causes. Bianchi (1992a) agrees with this assessment, but nevertheless offers Italy as an instructive example of both the best and the worst in industrial policy-making. National government in Italy constructed a policy for the Mezzogiorno (the South) that ignored regional governments and proceeded to pump in enormous subsidies to the giant industrial enterprises of the North in order to encourage them to set up large capital-intensive plants in the South. This was a complete failure and Italy was the only country in Europe to have increased internal regional disparities in recent history.[6] At the same time, however, a regional and local industrial strategy was dramatically succeeding in the Third Italy where dependence on handouts from national government had been avoided. Here a much more subtle process of endogenous economic development involving networks of innovators was being supported by the provision of '... information, training, research facilities and entry opportunities to final markets ...' (Bianchi 1992a). This sort of policy clearly does not constitute an interregional zero-sum game with the more successful regions absorbing resources from outside; rather it is a process by which a regionally indigenous, latent economic dynamism can be released.

However, this experience, seen in its extreme form in Italy, with its extremely large state aid to industry, has been, and is being observed throughout Europe, and while Union policy is containing largesse in the support of large enterprises, it is at the same time supporting the development of the more effective industrial strategy which appears in the regions. For example, the new industrial policy based on the 'balanced development' of the Single Market identifies as one set of policies public support for the development of small companies through the promotion of a network of innovators (see Commission 1990), and the Reform of Structural Funds (Commission 1989) sought to bring 'the regions into play as primary actors in the policy-making process' (Bianchi 1992b). There remains the critical question of the significance attached to this aspect of policy-making by both those at the Commission and those operating policy-making within the member states, but the structure is certainly there for a regionally based industrial strategy focused on creating a local industrial dynamism based on the development of networks of indigenous entrepreneurs. This focus receives support from research on regional development; for instance, Sweeney (1985) concludes: 'entrepreneurial vitality is very much a local phenomenon. Prosperity and economic growth of regions and localities are strongly associated with the strength and vitality of the small firm sector in the region or locality'.

Thus, whilst the development of Union policy could be seen as an increasingly constraining force in terms of the traditional industrial policy-making of nation states, as has been observed in Italy and indeed Britain in recent years (for example, over the sale of British Leyland), in terms of the approach to industrial strategy advocated in this book it is, to some degree, congruent. For member states in general, and Britain in particular, our approach to industrial strategy warrants some shift in power from national governments to Brussels and from national governments to the regions. Clearly national governments within the Union have varied in the degree of their acquiescence to both Union policy and, even more so, to regional autonomy, so that the extent of the shift required will vary substantially across member states. for example, Britain, at one and the same time, has been slow to accept both Union authority and regional autonomy, whereas Germany appears to have been much more willing to share power, and there are clear historical and political reasons why this is so. Nevertheless, in general a shift to Brussels would seem appropriate as a change necessary to facilitate the containment of the power of transnationals which are already operating at least at a European level (see Sharp 1993). Clearly, there is a distinct possibility that the policy-making apparatus in Brussels will be captured by corporate interests; indeed, the 1992 project can be seen as their creation (see Ramsay 1990). This real possibility has to be countered by the development of effective democratic control over the Commission; the creation of effective parliamentary institutions at Union level is clearly a centrally important objective that should take precedence over the narrow monetary concerns which presently take centre stage in the post-Maastricht period. A decisive move from the charade of the present European Parliament to an effective European political democracy is fraught with difficulties but ultimately attainable, and should not deter us from seeking a Union-wide strategy on the transnationals. Similarly with the regions: the shift of policy-making to the regions is a necessary condition for achieving more diffuse, deconcentrated and therefore dynamic economies. The scenario is of national economies made up of meaningful regional economies, and regions populated with closely interrelated enterprises with an indigenous base, rather than dominated by branch plants of far-distant parent companies with few linkages with other enterprises within the region (Sabel 1988).

The direct, political connection of the regions with Brussels, and with other regions, is also a desirable objective in its own right, serving as it will to establish the significance of a wider democracy, a wider community. This would be an outward-looking rather than introverted approach, a matter of equity, in that complete regional autonomy within Europe could lead to an increasing divergence between rich and poor. It would also be a matter of efficiency, given that introverted societies can lose impetus and momentum without the stimuli of outside influences. Thus in Europe, and of course else-where, industrial policy must be regional policy, inspired and created within the regions, but regional policy must be coherent as a whole, at the interregional level, and common desires across regions should be pursued collectively, for example, via international networks between European regions. Such developments provide further justi-fication for the existence of a supranational policy aimed at containing the ability of transnational corporations to play off regions against each other. A particularly acute problem of transnational power appears outside the Union but within the wider Europe. The present transition of the formerly centrally administered economies of the East leaves them particularly vulnerable to the transnationals, whose investment they presently seek. Establishing control over the transna-tionals within this wider Europe is crucial if the exploitation of this present vulnerability is to be avoided. Thus the increasing involve-ment of Brussels in developments to the East, which are likely to cul-minate in a much wider membership of the Union, should urgently include a strategy on the transnationals operating in that wider con-text. In addition, the linking-in of regions in the East with Brussels and with regions in the Union should be encouraged. This would put the whole process of economic integration on to a more diffuse and disaggregated basis and in itself would act as a counter to the other-wise highly centralized process which connects Brussels with poten-tial member states to the East. The fact that these nation states were, in recent history at least, tightly administered from the centre adds greater force to the argument: as a matter of central policy, mean-ingful regional economies were displaced by monocultures and this situation can only be reversed by a sharp refocusing of policy within a wider European context, for example, by bringing in the lessons learned in places like Emilia-Romagna, Baden Württemberg and Western Jutland.

Drawing the threads together

In the light of the lack of dynamism and the associated persistent unemployment throughout most of the present world economy, we would suggest urgent attention be given to the significant gap in policy-making which is generally evident, the construction of an industrial strategy. We have sought to identify a new approach to industrial strategy based on an examination of some fundamental deficiencies of free market economies as they have developed in the twentieth century. Our approach diverges from previous approaches for a quite fundamental reason: previous approaches to policy-making in this area start with markets and the consideration of market failure, whereas we choose to start with the modern corporation and a consideration of the socially incomplete nature of strategic decision-making within it. In the absence of purposive government policy aimed at changing matters, we see the long-term evolution of free market economies as dictated by the strategic decisions of large and dominating organizations — the transnationally based, major corporations. It is the concentration of decision-making power within the upper reaches of these organizations that shapes the character of the market, on both the supply side and the demand side, that is, in terms of shaping the global pattern of consumption as well as the global pattern of production, as we have sought to establish. To remedy defects in the free market economy we must seek to change the nature of strategic decision-making within the modern corporation, and in the longer term seek to displace its dominance within the market system. It is this process whereby a concentrated structure of decision-making within the industrial economy is progressively replaced by a democratic structure that constitutes the essence of industrial strategy-making, given our identification of the defects of the free market system. Such a strategy will inevitably require the development of appropriate agency structures, various forms of government, both reflecting and informing the democratic policy, at local, regional, national and supranational level.

We have applied our general principles to the task of both evaluating current policy and prescribing appropriate policy in the context of a variety of central and topical issues — privatisation, inward investment, technology, Europe and the regions. In the case of both privatization and inward investment we have identified severe deficiencies in past and present policies, but this is not meant to deny their potential relevance to industrial strategy. Rather, what we argue for is the necessity of their incorporation within a broader strategy in which a broader array of interests are represented. Thus the process of privatization needs to be embedded within appropriate sectoral strategies and needs to be coupled with an effort to open up strategy-making within each major corporation involved, both by restructuring and by changing the nature of decision-making within what remains. So it is with the case of inward investment. Whilst we would wish to emphasize the importance of endogenous development created by a flourishing network of small, indigenous enterprises, we recognize that inward investment can be an important stimulus to dynamism. However, if the aim at certain stages of development is to bring in foreign transnational corporations with certain, for example, technological expertise, then it is important, if the potential benefits are to be fully realized, that attention is given to linking in the new entrant to the domestic technology complex, as is done in Japan. In the case of technology policy more generally, we have advocated the creation of new structures designed to support systems of small-scale production, part of an extended infrastructure dedicated to achieving a gradual but persistent and fundamental change in industrial structures over an extended time period. Finally, our consideration of the European, and particularly Italian experience suggests both the real opportunities offered by endogenous development at regional level and the failure of traditional state aid operated at national level. These observations fit quite securely within our framework of analysis, supporting as they do our contention that industrial strategy should be founded on strong regional roots and that simply doling out state aid to the dominant organizations of the existing industrial structure is not only wasteful but holds back necessary change.

The above illustrations should serve to emphasize that rather than being simply critical of existing policies, and pessimistic about the development of more effective policies in these areas, we are seeking more positive and proactive solutions, solutions which start with fundamentals. Our analysis has started with the large-scale corporation, specifically the Anglo-American corporation. This is not simply a mid-Atlantic parochialism on our part: the US form of the capitalist firm became the dominant form of organization within twentieth-century capitalism, and indeed the dominant form also within the so-called socialist economies. Nevertheless, we have also argued that our analysis retains its validity in the increasingly important case of the Japanese firm, as in cases where imperfect adaptations along Japanese lines have been made within the West. Nor do we see our analysis undermined by organizational developments within the major corporations which may have been learnt from very different production systems characterized by networks of small-scale units. But we do see this alternative and fundamentally different system of production, which has over the past twenty years or so revealed itself capable of emerging and competing with the dominant mode, as offering great hope for the future.

The industrial district, this alternative non-hierarchical system, and the large vertically integrated corporation are quite distinct modes of production, the former being characterized by essentially symmetric relationships and the latter, no matter what the nature of reorganisation, preserving a hierarchical or asymmetric set of relationships between its constituent parts. As Dei Ottati (1991) has argued, ' ... the quality of intersubjective relations is different in the two forms of organisation'. We see the shifting of the boundaries between the domains of the major corporations and the industrial districts in favour of the latter as a feasible and necessary step on the path to economic democracy. That this needs to be done as a matter of purposive policy rather than evolving naturally in a process of free competition between alternative systems does not deny the efficiency of the industrial district; rather it reflects a realistic assessment of the power of the major corporations. A truly devolved and democratic system of decision-making cannot be achieved without challenging this power base. Our analysis has exposed the incompatibility between democracy and capitalism. Thus we can never approach economic democracy without necessarily transforming the system. The process can begin within capitalism but, if it is pursued to its logical end, will result in a system which can no longer be accurately defined as capitalism. Whereabouts along this trajectory of change existing industrial districts should be placed is not entirely clear and indeed we would need the views of those directly involved to begin to make such a judgement. But, from an external vantage point, it seems clear that within the industrial districts of the Third Italy, the distinction between public and private, employer and employee are nowhere near as sharp as they tend to be elsewhere. But whether we see what exists as a species of the genus capitalism, or something different, is not a big issue. Within our framework the institution of the modern industrial district, of which we have identified examples, simply offers an example of something better to which we can realistically aspire within the near future. How far we might wish to go in replicating what has been achieved, rather than being inspired by it, and how far we would wish to go beyond what has been achieved are matters for democratic debate. But we do see what has been achieved in these various regions as something that is important in both focusing that debate and indeed in helping to get it off the ground. Most people can move only so far in terms of abstract arguments; concrete examples of a better world can inspire people to look beyond their present, and often pressing circumstances.

Finally, there is the question of the broader international dimension of our analysis and proposals. Whilst we have argued that our analysis of deficiencies of the free market economy, centring as it does on the Anglo-American corporation, does not in itself betray our parochialism, the same cannot be maintained for the focus of our policy discussion. However, although we shall not deal with it at any length in this book, we do feel our analysis has a much wider resonance in the framing of economic policy than the essentially European focus we have adopted.[7] Indeed, we see the deficiencies of free market economies as being most evident within the context of those countries which remain significantly underdeveloped, and in those economies on the eastern side of Europe and beyond currently suffering the ravages of an unplanned transition to free market economies. Our call for the creation of democratic market economies, and thus the requirement for the construction of industrial strategies to steer these economies in that direction, we see as having a general validity. This leads us into a position of sharp opposition to the major existing supranational policy institution — the International Monetary Fund/World Bank axis — which demands total acceptance of free market conditions for their support (see Avramovic 1988 and Singh 1992). It has been put to us in private conversation with someone negotiating with them that it is the position of the IMF/World Bank axis that is the fundamental explanation for the apparent lack of interest in industrial strategy across Central and Eastern Europe and the countries of the former Soviet Union. This is a remarkable situation, and also a deeply depressing one. Aid is being linked to democracy, political not economic, and also, crucially, to access to markets and the decline of the state as an economic actor, in the same way as the IMF/World Bank has worked *vis-à-vis* the Third World. That programme is inappropriate for the Third World because the development of modern economies out of relatively backward economies needs some degree of isolation from the forces of the free market and requires a modernizing proactive state, with the East Asian economies offering powerful examples of the success that can be achieved. For related reasons, the IMF/World Bank programme is also inappropriate for Central and Eastern Europe and the countries of the former Soviet Union. Its inappropriateness is, moreover, compounded in this case by the inexpertness with the market, which must be true of Central and Eastern Europe, but which is especially true in a deeper, historical sense for the countries of the former Soviet Union. Not only that, but the more advanced countries will also suffer as a result of the almost inevitable dislocation this induces. What is required is that the necessary industrial restructuring to the East takes place within a controlled approach to trade liberalization. The solution would appear to be neither Big Bang nor Gradualism, the two alternatives around which the debate has centred, but rather a subtle mixture of the two: decisive restructuring within a system of managed trade. But rather than trade being managed by the transnationals, trade management would be effected by the countries themselves, just as in the case of the Japanese or the Koreans. As Keynes (1933) argued, 'we all need to be as free as possible of interference from economic changes elsewhere, in order to make our own favourite experiments towards the ideal social republic of the future'. The debate on the transformation has become too compressed, and it appears that the powerful agency of the IMF/World Bank has played a significant part in this process of compression.

We now turn to the Third World. This book has been concerned to demonstrate the serious and fundamental deficiencies of the free market system, but it is exactly this system the IMF/World Bank is actively seeking to create and sustain within the Third World. Inevitably the policy proposals — privatization, deregulation, liberalization and closer integration with the world economy — will be subject to serious flaws, given that they are advocated without regard to the extension of democratic control and apparently without recognition, or more likely concern, that such policies, without being integrated into a broader strategy to secure a more diffuse and deconcentrated structure of strategic decision-making, will simply sustain and enhance the present dominance of the transnational giants. Policies which appear at first sight to be liberating in character have the opposite effect. Attempts by communities throughout the world to construct their own futures are being swamped by the global extension of the power of the transnationals aided and abetted by the policies adopted by the IMF/World Bank. An élitist system of decision-making within the free market economy is being supported by a similar structure of decision-making in world government. Nothing less than the complete reversal of such policies is called for.

So, in a nutshell, what does it all add up to? What are we saying about the world economy and what are we proposing? We presently live in a world where economic life is dominated by a relatively few, very large private organizations with a global presence interacting with national governments and supra-national governmental institutions, some of which have considerable economic power. The crucial characteristic of the former group is that each of its members, each major corporation, is controlled by a small minority of those connected with it or influenced by it. The crucial, present characteristic of the latter group is that although some of its members, national governments or supra-national government institutions, have considerable potential leverage within the market economy, by and large, they choose not to use it in any systemic way: they rely on the former group, the central institutions of the free market economy, to determine a vision for the economy and to set the strategy for moving towards that vision. The present condition of the world economy reflects that structure of the use of power. We have argued for its radical restructuring. As we see it, the clear deficiencies of the present system can only be remedied by democratizing the structure of strategic decision-making within the economy; it requires the creation of an economic democracy. The process of transformation from a free market economy to a democratic market economy requires the present concentrated structure of decision-making be replaced by one which is diffuse and deconcentrated. The thrust of industrial economic strategy should be guided by this desired end. Its achievement will require a new, proactive and creative role be adopted by government, which will in turn be dependent on radical change within government. The creation of a new and better world economic order demands that the concentration of power within the economy and within the nation state be challenged and replaced by something that can be accurately described as a full democracy. We hope this book has provided a signpost for the way forward.

Notes

1 Cowling (1994) offers a fuller treatment of the issue.
2 Clearly, Austrian economics presumes to offer a theoretical case, but see how Devine (1993) has turned this on its head; it would seem implausible that entrepreneurialism is uniquely a characteristic of capitalist enterprise.
3 Such tragedies are features of both central planning and monopoly capitalism, as is clear from the undevelopment of many countries incorporated within the market system; witness much of Africa and Latin America.
4 As we have noted before, the attention given to the market rather than the organization is also a feature of the mainstream of our profession. It is as if there were no wish to know how superior organizations are created.
5 The idea has now taken hold outside the Third Italy, for example, in Coventry, England where a similar Clothing Resource Centre has been set up in recent years.
6 The recent assessment of industrial policy-making in Ireland, following similar principles except that the investment came from outside Ireland, comes to similar conclusions about Ireland, as we have already observed (Kennedy et al. 1992).

7 In the present context of the Maastricht treaty, the recent GATT agreement, the emergence of the North American Free Trade Area (NAFTA) and the 1993 agreement between two major trading blocs (the United States and the East Asian economies), all based on a belief in the efficiency of a free market system, it may appear to the reader that our proposals are cutting across the grain of historical development and are therefore wildly unrealistic. Our view would be that these various developments, unless grounded within a strategy for democratising strategic-decision making, will inevitably founder. We see no successful future based on the extension of the free market system and this will become increasingly apparent, partly as a result of the changes in the organization of the world economy just identified. Such failures could provide a productive seed-bed for the planting of new ideas about the appropriate way forward, provided such new ideas have been adequately analyzed and thought through.

REFERENCES

Ádám, Gyorgy, 1975, 'Multinational corporations and worldwide sourcing', in Hugo Radice (ed.), *International firms and modern imperialism*, London, Penguin.

Adams, W. and Brock, J., 1988, 'The bigness mystique and the merger policy debate: an international perspective', *Northwestern Journal of International Law and Business*, 9, 1–48.

Aharoni, Y., 1971, 'On the definition of a multinational corporation', *Quarterly Review of Economics and Business*, 11, 27–37.

Alchian, A.A. and Demsetz, H., 1972, 'Production, information costs and economic organization', *American Economic Review*, 62, 777–96.

Amin, A. and Dietrich, M., 1991, *Towards a new Europe? Structural change in the European economy*, Gloucester, Edward Elgar.

Amsden, A., 1989, *Asia's next giant: South Korea and late industrialization*, New York, Oxford University Press.

Anchordoghy, M., 1988, 'Mastering the market: Japanese government targeting of the computer industry', *International Organisation*, 42, 509–43.

Aoki, Masahiko, 1990a, 'The participatory generation of information rents and the theory of the firm', in Masahiko Aoki, Bo Gustafsson and Oliver E. Williamson (eds), *The firm as a nexus of treaties*, London, Sage.

Aoki, Masahiko, 1990b, 'Toward an economic model of the Japanese firm', *Journal of Economic Literature*, XXVIII, 1–27.

Attaran, M. and Saghafi, M., 1988, 'Concentration trends and profitability in the US manufacturing sector 1970–84', *Applied Economics*, 20, 1497–1510.

Avramovic, D., 1988, *Conditionality: facts, theory and policy-contribution to the reconstruction of the international financial system*, Helsinki,

World Institute of Development Economic Research (WIDER).

Bailey, David, Harte, George and Sugden, Roger, 1994, *Transnationals and governments: recent policies in Japan, France, Germany, the United States and Britain*, London, Routledge.

Baran, Paul A. and Sweezy, Paul M., 1966, *Monopoly capital*, Harmondsworth, Penguin.

Barnet, Richard J. and Müller, Ronald E., 1974, *Global reach*, New York, Simon & Schuster.

Benson, I. and Lloyd, J., 1983, *New technology and industrial change*, London, Kogan Page.

Best, M., 1990, *The new competition: institutions of industrial restructuring*, Cambridge, Polity Press.

Bhaduri, A. and Steindl, J., 1983, 'The rise of monetarism as a social doctrine', *Thames Papers in Political Economy*.

Bianchi, Patrizio, 1992a, 'Experience in Italy', in Keith Cowling and Roger Sugden (eds), *Current issues in industrial economic strategy*, Manchester, Manchester University Press.

Bianchi, Patrizio, 1992b, 'Industrial Strategy and Structural Policies', in Keith Cowling and Roger Sugden (eds), *Current issues in industrial economic strategy*, Manchester, Manchester University Press.

Bils, M., 1987, 'The cyclical behaviour of marginal cost and price', *American Economic Review*, 77, 838–55.

Blackaby, F., 1979, *Deindustrialization*, London, Heinemann.

Blanchard, O. and Layard, R., 1991, 'How to privatise', *London School of Economics Centre for Economic Performance Discussion Paper*, Number 50.

Blanchflower, David, 1984, 'Comparative pay levels in domestically-owned manufacturing plants: a comment', *British Journal of Industrial Relations*, XXII, 265–7.

Blinder, A., 1988, 'The challenge of high unemployment', *American Economic Review*, 78, 1–15.

Borensztein, E., 1993, 'The strategy of reform in the centrally planned economies of Eastern Europe: lessons and challenges', *Papers on policy Analysis and Assessment*, Washington, DC, IMF.

Brusco, S., 1982, 'The Emilian model', *Cambridge Journal of Economics*, 6, 167–84.

Buckley, Peter J. and Casson, Mark, 1976, *The future of the multinational enterprise*, London, Macmillan.

Buckley, Peter J. and Enderwick, Peter, 1983, 'Comparative pay levels in domestically-owned and foreign-owned plants in UK manufacturing: evidence from the 1980 Workplace Industrial Relations Survey', *British Journal of Industrial Relations*, XXI, 395–400.

Burkitt, Brian and Bowers, David, 1979, *Trade unions and the economy*, London, Macmillan.

CEPR, 1990, *Monitoring European integration: the impact of Eastern Europe*, London, Centre for Economic and Policy Research.

Charkham, J., 1989, 'Corporate governance and the market for control of companies', *Bank of England Panel Paper*, 25.

Chen, E., 1979, *Hypergrowth in Asian economies: a comparative survey of Hong Kong, Japan, Singapore and Taiwan*, London, Macmillan.

CIS, 1978, *Anti-report: the Ford Motor Company*, Anti-report Number 20, Counter Information Services.

Coase, Ronald H., 1937, 'The nature of the firm', *Economica*, IV, 386–405.

Coase, Ronald H., 1991, 'The nature of the firm: influence', in Oliver E. Williamson and Sidney G. Winter (eds), *The nature of the firm: origins, evolution and development*, Oxford, Oxford University Press.

Commission of the European Communities, 1989, *Primo Censimento degli Aiuti di Stato nella Communità Europea*, Brussels.

Commission of the European Communities, 1990, 'Industrial policy in an open and competitive environment: guidelines for a community approach', Working Paper, Brussels.

Conyon, M., 1992, 'Monopoly capitalism, profits, income distribution and unionism', Ph.D. thesis, University of Warwick.

Cosh, A., Hughes, A. and Rowthorn, R. E., 1993, 'The competitive role of UK manufacturing industry, 1950–2003: a case analysis', *Cambridge/Harvard Project on Manufacturing Competitiveness*, University of Cambridge.

Cosh, A., Hughes, A., Singh, A., Carty, J. and Plender, J., 1990, 'Takeovers and short-termism in the UK', *Industrial Policy Paper*, Number 3, London, Institute for Public Policy Research.

Council for Science and Society, 1981, *New technology: society, employment and skill*, London, Blackrose Press.

Cowling, Keith, 1982, *Monopoly capitalism*, London, Macmillan.

Cowling, Keith, 1983, 'Excess capacity and the degree of collusion: oligopoly behaviour in the slump', *Manchester School*, 341–59.

Cowling, Keith, 1986, 'The internationalization of production and deindustrialization', in A. Amin and J. Goddard (eds), *Technological change, industrial restructuring and regional development*, London, Allen & Unwin.

Cowling, Keith, 1990, 'A new industrial strategy: preparing Europe for the turn of the century', *International Journal of Industrial Organization*, 8, 165–84.

Cowling, Keith, 1991, 'The modern European corporation: transnational and decentralised?', in D. Sadowski and O. Jacobi (eds), *Employers' associations in Europe: policy and organisation*, Baden-Baden, Nomos.

Cowling, Keith, 1994, 'The issue of privatisation', in Peter Nolan (ed.), *Reforming the centrally planned economies: critical essays*, London, Macmillan.

Cowling, Keith and Molho, Ian, 1982, 'Wage share, concentration and unionism', *Manchester School*, L.

Cowling, Keith and Naylor, Robin, 1992, 'Norms, sovereignty and regulation', *Metroeconomica*, 43, 177–204.

Cowling, Keith and Sugden, Roger, 1987, *Transnational monopoly capitalism*, Brighton, Wheatsheaf.

Cowling, Keith and Sugden, Roger, 1989, 'Exchange rate adjustment and oligopoly pricing behaviour', *Cambridge Journal of Economics*, 13, 373–93.

Cowling, Keith and Sugden, Roger, 1990, *A new economic policy for Britain: essays on the development of industry*, Manchester, Manchester University Press.

Cowling, Keith and Sugden, Roger, 1993a, 'Behind the market façade: an assessment and development of the theory of the firm', *Warwick Economic Research Papers*, Number 413, University of Warwick.

Cowling, Keith and Sugden, Roger, 1993b, 'Industrial development, markets and democratic processes: fostering technological change', *Occasional Papers in Industrial Strategy*, Number 12, Research Centre for Industrial Strategy, University of Birmingham.

Cowling, Keith and Sugden, Roger, 1993c, 'Industrial strategy: a missing link in British economic policy', *Oxford Review of Economic Policy*, 9, 83–100.

Crafts, N., 1985, *British economic growth during the Industrial Revolution*, Oxford, Oxford University Press.

Crafts, N., 1991, 'Reversing relative economic decline? The 1980s in historical perspective', *Oxford Review of Economic Policy*, 7, 81–98.

Cubbin, John and Leech, Dennis, 1983, 'The effects of shareholding dispersion on the degree of control in British companies', *Economic Journal*, 93, 351–69.

Cyert, R. M. and March, J. G., 1963, *A behavioral theory of the firm*, Englewood Cliffs, Prentice-Hall.

Davies, R., 1990, 'Gorbachov's socialism in historical perspective', *New Left Review*, January/February, 179.

Dei Ottati, G., 1991, 'The economic bases of diffuse industrialization', *International Studies of Management and Organization*, 21, 53–74.

Devine, P., 1993, 'Industrial strategy: process of content? Insights from the Austrians', Birmingham Workshop on *Industrial Economic*

Strategies for Europe: Preparing for the Turn of the Century, Research Centre for Industrial Strategy, University of Birmingham.

Dicken, Peter, 1986, *Global shift: industrial change in a turbulent world,* London, Harper & Row.

Dicken, Peter, 1992, *Global shift: the internationalization of economic activity,* London, Paul Chapman.

Dore, P., 1986, 'Industrial policy and how the Japanese do it', *Catalyst,* Spring, 45–58.

Dornbusch, R., Krugman, P. and Park, Y., 1989, *Meeting world challenges: US manufacturing in the 1990s,* Rochester, Eastman Kodak.

Dowrick, S., 1983, 'Notes on transnationals', mimeo, Department of Economics, University of Warwick.

Dowrick, S. and Gemmell, N., 1991, 'Industrialisation, catching up and economic growth', *Economic Journal* (Conference Volume).

Dunning, John H., 1980, 'Toward an eclectic theory of international production: some empirical tests', *Journal of International Business Studies,* 11, 9–31.

Dunning, John H., 1993, *Multinational enterprises and the global economy,* New York, Addison-Wesley.

Eads, G. C. and Yamamura, K., 1987, 'The future of industrial policy', in K. Yamamura and Y. Yasuba (eds), *The political economy of Japan, Volume 1,* Stanford, Stanford University Press.

Edwards, Corwin D., 1955, 'Conglomerate bigness as a source of power', National Bureau of Economic Research Conference Report, *Business concentration and price policy,* Princeton, NJ, Princeton University Press.

Edwards, Corwin D., 1979, 'The multimarket enterprise and economic power', *Journal of Economic Issues,* XII, 285–301.

Edwards, Richard, 1979, *Contested terrain,* London, Heinemann.

Eltis, W. and Fraser, D., 1992, 'The contribution of Japanese success to Britain and to Europe', *National Westminster Bank Quarterly Review,* November, 2–19.

Enderwick, Peter, 1985, *Multinational business and labour,* London, Croom Helm.

Feagin, Joe R. and Smith, Michael Peter, 1987, 'Cities and the new international division of labour: an overview', in M. P. Smith and J. R. Feagin (eds), *The capitalist city: global restructuring and community politics,* Oxford, Basil Blackwell.

Feinberg, Robert M., 1985, '"Sales-at-risk": a test of the mutual forbearance theory of conglomerate behaviour', *Journal of Business,* 58, 225–41.

Fishlow, A., 1991, 'Review of *Handbook of Development Economics*',

Journal of Economic Literature, XXIX, 1728–37.

Forsyth, David J. C., 1972, *US investment in Scotland*, Eastbourne, Praeger.

Frank, R., 1992, 'Melding sociology and economics: James Coleman's *Foundations of Social Theory*', *Journal of Economic Literature*, XXX, 147–70.

Freeman, R., 1988, 'Evaluating the European view that the United States has no employment problem', *American Economic Review*, 78, 294–9.

Friedman, Andrew L., 1977, *Industry and labour: class struggle at work and monopoly capitalism*, London, Macmillan.

Fröbel, Folker, Heinrichs, Jürgen and Kreye, Otto, 1980, *The new international division of labour*, Cambridge, Cambridge University Press.

Gaffikin, F. and Nickson, A., 1984, *Jobs crisis and the multinationals: deindustrialisation in the West Midlands*, Birmingham, Third World Books.

Gennard, John, 1972, *Multinational corporations and British labour: a review of attitudes and responses*, British-North American Committee.

Geroski, P., 1990, 'Encouraging investment in science and technology', in Keith Cowling and Roger Sugden (eds), *A new economic policy for Britain: essays on the development of industry*, Manchester, Manchester University Press.

Geroski, P. and Stewart, G., 1991, 'Competitive rivalry and the response of markets to innovative opportunities', in S. Arndt and G. W. McKenzie (eds), *The competitiveness of the UK economy*, London, Macmillan.

Glyn, A. and Rowthorn, R. E., 1988, 'West European unemployment: corporatism and structural change', *American Economic Review*, 78, 194–9.

Goldthorpe, J., 1984, *Order and conflict in contemporary capitalism*, Oxford, Clarendon Press.

Gomulka, S., 1991, 'Polish economic reform: principles, policies and surprises', *London School of Economics Centre for Economic Performance Discussion Paper*, Number 51.

Gordon, R., 1992, 'Discussion of N. Crafts, *Productivity Growth Reconsidered*', *Economic Policy*, October, 414–21.

Greer, Charles R. and Shearer, John C., 1981, 'Do foreign-owned US firms practise unconventional labour relations?', *Monthly Labour Review*, 104, 44–8.

Grosfeld, I., 1990, 'Prospects for privatisation in Poland', *European Economy*, 43, 141–50.

Hare, P., 1985, *Planning the British economy*, London, Macmillan.

Harte, George and Sugden, Roger, 1990, 'A proposal for monitoring transnational corporations', in Keith Cowling and Roger Sugden (eds), *A new economic policy for Britain: essays on the development of industry*, Manchester, Manchester University Press.

Helfgott, Ray B., 1983, 'American unions and multinational companies: a case of misplaced emphasis', *Columbia Journal of World Business*, 18, 81–6.

Helleiner, G. K. and Lavergne, R., 1979, 'Intra-firm trade and industrial exports to the United States', *Oxford Bulletin of Economics and Statistics*, 41, 297–312.

Hennart, Jean-François, 1991, 'The transaction cost theory of the multinational enterprise', in Christos Pitelis and Roger Sugden (eds), *The nature of the transnational firm*, London, Routledge.

Heseltine, M., 1987, *Where there's a will*, London, Hutchinson.

House of Commons, 1992, *Energy Committee: Second Report, Volume 1*, London, HMSO.

House of Lords Select Committee on Science and Technology, 1988, *Civil Research and Development*, HLLO, London, HMSO.

Hymer, Stephen H., 1960, *The international operations of national firms* (published in 1976), Cambridge, Mass., MIT Press.

Hymer, Stephen H., 1972, 'The multinational corporation and the law of uneven development', in J. N. Bhagwati (ed.), *Economics and world order*, London, Macmillan.

ILO, 1976a, *Multinationals in Western Europe: the industrial relations experience*, Geneva, International Labour Office.

ILO, 1976b, *Wages and working conditions in multinational enterprises*, Geneva, International Labour Office.

Jenkinson, Tim and Mayer, Colin, 1992, 'The assessment: corporate governance and corporate control', *Oxford Review of Economic Policy*, 8, 1–10.

Johnson, C., 1982, *MITI and the Japanese miracle: the growth of industrial policy 1925–75*, Stanford, Stanford University Press.

Johnson, C., 1984, *The industrial policy debate*, Stanford, Institute for Contemporary Studies Press.

Kalecki, Michál, 1971, *Dynamics of the capitalist economy*, Cambridge, Cambridge University Press.

Kaletsky, A., 1993, 'Labour Party remains the last bastion of monetarism', *The Times*, 19 August, 25.

Keir, T., 1993, 'The aggregate advertising-consumption relationship revisited', M.Sc. dissertation, Department of Economics, University of Warwick.

Kennedy, K., Giblin, T. and McHugh, D., 1992, *The economic development of Ireland in the twentieth century*, London, Routledge.

Keynes, J., 1933, 'National self-sufficiency', *New Statesman and Nation*.

Kindleberger, Charles P., 1969, *American business abroad*, New Haven, Yale University Press.

Knickerbocker, Frederick T., 1973, *Oligopolistic reaction and multinational enterprises*, Boston, Harvard Business School.

Knight, K. G. and Sugden, Roger, 1990, 'Efficiency, economic democracy and company law', in K. Cowling and R. Sugden (eds), *A new economic policy for Britain: essays on the development of industry*, Manchester, Manchester University Press.

Kobayashi, Y., 1993, 'The role and significance of Japanese industrial policy', *Warwick Economic Research Paper*, Number 404, University of Warwick.

Koike, Kazuo, 1990, 'Intellectual skill and the role of employees as constituent members of large firms in contemporary Japan', in Masahiko Aoki, Bo Gustafson and Oliver E. Williamson (eds), *The firm as a nexus of treaties*, London, Sage.

Koo, A. and Martin, S., 1984, 'Market structure and US trade flows', *International Journal of Industrial Organization*, 2, 25–42.

Kornai, J., 1990, *The road to freedom*, New York, Norton.

Koutsoyiannis, A., 1982, *Non-price decisions*, London, Macmillan.

Kowalik, T., 1991, 'Privatization and social participation: the Polish case', *Workshop on Participation and Change in Property Relations in East-Central Europe and the Soviet Union*, The Hague.

Krause, L. B. and Ney, J. S., 1975, 'Reflections on the economics and politics of international economic organizations', in C. F. Bergsten and L. B. Krause (eds), *World politics and international economics*, Washington, DC, Brookings Institution.

Kristensen, P., 1990, 'Education, technical culture and regional prosperity in Denmark', in G. Sweeney, T. Casey, P. Kristensen and Noe R. Prujai (eds), *Education, technical culture and regional prosperity*, Dublin, SICA.

Krugman, P., 1987, 'Is free trade passé?', *Journal of Economic Perspectives*, 1, 131–44.

Labour Party, 1993, *Making Britain's future*, London, Labour Party.

Lewchuk, W., 1986, 'The motor vehicle industry', in B. Elbaum and W. Lazonick (eds), *The decline of the British economy*, Oxford, Clarendon Press.

Lim, C., 1988, 'Taiwan's economic miracle: a Singaporean perspective', mimeo, Department of Economics, University of Singapore.

Lim, L., 1983, 'Singapore's success: the myth of the market', *Asian Survey*, XVII, 73–94.

Little, I., 1979, 'An economic renaissance', in W. Galerson (ed.), *Economic growth and structural change in Taiwan: the postwar experience of the Republic of China*, Ithaca, Cornell University Press.

Lively, T., 1975, *Democracy*, Oxford, Basil Blackwell.

Löhn, J. and Stadelmeier, M., 1990, 'The Baden-Württemberg model of technology transfer', in K. Cowling and H. Tomann (eds), *Industrial policy after 1992: an Anglo-German perspective*, London, Anglo-German Foundation.

Lombardini, S., 1992, 'Privatization in market economies and for building a market economy', in F. Targetti (ed.), *Privatization in Europe: West and East experiences*, Aldershot, Dartmouth.

McPherson, Michael, 1983, 'Efficiency and liberty in the productive enterprise: recent work in the economics of work organisation', *Philosophy and Public Affairs*, 12, 354–68.

Maizels, A., 1992, *Commodities in crisis*, Oxford, Clarendon Press.

Mandel, E., 1968, *Marxist economic theory*, London, Merlin.

Marchanté, A., 1987, 'An analysis of the relationship between corporate and personal savings, pooling cross-section and time series data of 13 OECD countries, 1964–1980', M.A. dissertation, University of Warwick.

Marginson, Paul, 1986, 'Labour and the modern corporation: mutual interest or control?', *Warwick Papers in Industrial Relations*, Number 9, University of Warwick.

Marglin, Stephen A., 1974, 'What do bosses do? The origins and functions of hierarchy in capitalist production', *Review of Radical Political Economics*, 6, 60–112.

Minns, Richard and Rogers, Mary, 1990, 'The state as public entrepreneur', in Keith Cowling and Roger Sugden (eds), *A new economic policy for Britain: essays on the development of industry*, Manchester, Manchester University Press.

Mitter, Swasti, 1986, 'Industrial restructuring and manufacturing homework: immigrant women in the UK clothing industry', *Capital and Class*, 27.

Neuburger, H., 1985, 'Planning the British economy: comment', *Economics of Planning*, 19, 160–5.

Nolan, P., 1991, 'State and market in the transition from Stalinism: Chinese economic reforms in comparative perspective', Conference of *The European Association for Research in Industrial Economics*, Ferrara.

Norton, R., 1986, 'Industrial policy and American renewal', *Journal of Economic Literature*, XXIV, 1–40.

Odagiri, H., 1992, *Growth through competition, competition through growth: strategic management and the economy of Japan*, Oxford, Clarendon Press.

Ozaki, R., 1984, 'Misperceptions of Japanese industrial policy', in C. Johnson, *MITI and the Japanese miracle*, Stanford, Stanford University Press.

Pavitt, K., Robson, M. and Townsend, J., 1987, 'Size distribution of innovating firms in the UK: 1945–1983', *Journal of Industrial Economics*, XXXV, 297–316.

Piore, M. and Sabel, C., 1984, *The second industrial divide: possibility for prosperity*, New York, Basic Books.

Pitelis, C., 1982, 'Business savings and the macroeconomic distribution of income: the "Monopoly Capitalism Savings Function"', *Warwick Economic Research Papers*, Number 219, University of Warwick.

Pitelis, C., 1986, *Corporate capital: control, ownership, saving and prices*, Cambridge, Cambridge University Press.

Pitelis, Christos and Sugden, Roger, 1986, 'The separation of ownership and control in the theory of the firm: a reappraisal', *International Journal of Industrial Organization*, 4, 69–86.

Pitt-Watson, David, 1991, *Economic short-termism: a cure for the British disease, Fabian Pamphlet*, Number 547, London, Fabian Society.

Pollard, S., 1982, *The wasting of the British economy*, London, Croom Helm.

Pollard, S., 1992, 'Review of N. Crafts and N. Woodward (eds), *The British Economy Since 1945*', *Economic Journal*, 102, 1282–4.

Porter, M., 1987, *Competition in global industries*, London, Macmillan.

Porter, M., 1990, *The competitive advantage of nations*, London, Macmillan.

Ramsay, H., 1990, '1992: the year of the multinational? Corporate restructuring and labour in the Single Market', *Warwick Papers in Industrial Relations*, Number 35, University of Warwick.

Ranis, G., 1979, 'Industrial development', in W. Galerson (ed.), *Economic growth and structural change in Taiwan: the postwar experience of the Republic of China*, Ithaca, Cornell University Press.

Reich, R., 1983, *The next American frontier*, Harmondsworth, Penguin.

Reich, R., 1991, *The work of nations*, New York, Knopf.

Rothschild, K., 1942, 'A note on advertising', *Economic Journal*, April.

Rowthorn, R. E. and Wells, T., 1987, *Deindustrialisation and foreign trade*, Cambridge, Cambridge University Press.

Sabel, C., 1988, 'The re-emergence of regional economies', *Papers de Seminari*, 29–30, 71–140.

Scherer, F. M., 1980, *Industrial market structure and economic performance*, Chicago, Rand-McNally.

Scherer, F. M. and Ross, David, 1990, *Industrial market structure and economic performance*, Boston, Houghton Mifflin.

Scitovsky, T., 1980, 'Can capitalism survive? An old question in a new setting', *American Economic Review*, 70, 1–9.

Sen, Amantya, 1993, 'Capability and well-being', in Martha Nussbaum and Amantya Sen (eds), *The quality of life*, Oxford, Clarendon Press.

Sharp, M., 1993, 'Industrial policy and globalization: what role for the nation state?', PSI Conference on *The Future of UK Industrial Competitiveness*, London.

Sharp, M. and Shepherd, G., 1987, *Managing change in British industry*, Geneva, International Labour Organization.

Simon, Herbert A., 1959, 'Theories of decision-making in economics and behavioral science', *American Economic Review*, 49, 253–83.

Simon, Herbert A., 1991, 'Organizations and markets', *Journal of Economic Perspectives*, 5, 25–44.

Singh, A., 1992, 'Industrial policy in the Third World in the 1990s: alternative perspectives', in Keith Cowling and Roger Sugden (eds), *Current issues in industrial economic strategy*, Manchester, Manchester University Press.

Singh, A., 1993, 'Asian economic success and Latin American failure in the 1980s: new analyses and future policy implications', *International Review of Applied Economics*, 7, 267–89.

Steindl, J., 1952, *Maturity and stagnation in American capitalism*, Oxford, Oxford University Press.

Steindl, J., 1966, 'On maturity in capitalist economies', in *Problems of economic dynamics and planning: essays in honour of Michal Kalecki*, Oxford, Pergamon Press.

Steindl, J., 1990, 'From stagnation in the 1930s to slow growth in the 1970s', in M. Berg (ed.), *Political economy in the twentieth century*, London, Philip Allen.

Steinherr, A., 1991, 'Essential ingredients for reforms in Eastern Europe', *European Journal on Eastern Europe and the Soviet Union*, 3, 3–28.

Steuer, Max and Gennard, John, 1971, 'Industrial relations, labour disputes and labour utilisation in foreign-owned firms in the United Kingdom', in John H. Dunning (ed), *The multinational enterprise*, London, Allen & Unwin.

Stewart, G., 1983, 'Workers cooperatives and the alternative economic strategy', in M. Sawyer and K. Schott (eds), *Socialist economic review*, London, Merlin.

Stigler, G., 1968, *The organization of industry*, Homewood, Irwin.

Stoneman, P. and Vickers, J., 1988, 'The assessment: the economics of technology policy', *Oxford Review of Economic Policy*, 4, i–xvi.

Stopford, John M. and Turner, Louis, 1985, *Britain and the multinationals*,

Chichester, Wiley-IRM.

Sugden, Roger, 1989, 'The warm welcome for foreign owned transnationals from recent British governments', in Martin Chick (ed.), *Government-industry relations post-1945*, Gloucester, Edward Elgar.

Sugden, Roger, 1990, 'Strategic industries, community control and transnational corporations', *International Review of Applied Economics*, 4, 72–94.

Summers, R. and Heston, A., 1991, 'The Penn World Table (Mark 5): an expanded set of international comparisons, 1950–1988', *Quarterly Journal of Economics*, 327–68.

Sweeney, G., 1985, 'Innovation is entrepreneur-led', in G. Sweeney (ed.), *Innovation policies: an international perspective*, London, Pinter.

Sweeney, G., 1992a, 'Comportamenti conflittuali, concorrenti e collusivi nel policymaking: intervento', in C. Tolmelli (ed.), *Le politiche industriali regionali: Esperienze, Soggetti, Modelli*, Bologna, Clueb.

Sweeney, G., 1992b, 'The role of vocational training in endogenous economic growth', in J. Davis (ed.), *Education, training and local economic development*, Dublin, Regional Studies Association (Irish Branch).

Thomas, H., 1982, 'The performance of the Mondragon cooperatives in Spain', in D. Jones and J. Svejnar (eds), *Participatory and self-managed firms*, Lexington, Heath.

Turok, I., 1993, 'Loose connections? Foreign investment and local linkage in Silicon Glen', *Strathclyde Papers on Planning*, University of Strathclyde.

United Nations, 1992, *World investment report 1992, transnational corporations as engines of growth*, New York, United Nations.

United Nations, 1993, *World investment report 1993, transnational corporations and integrated international production*, New York, United Nations.

Vernon, Raymond, 1977, *Storm over the multinationals*, London, Macmillan.

Vernon, Raymond, 1979, 'The product cycle hypothesis in a new international environment', *Oxford Bulletin of Economics and Statistics*, 41, 255–67.

Vickers, J. and Yarrow, G., 1988, *Privatization and economic analysis*, Cambridge, Mass., MIT Press.

Vickers, J. and Yarrow, G., 1991, 'Economic perspectives on privatization', *Journal of Economic Perspectives*, 5, 111–32.

Wade, R., 1990a, *Governing the market: economic theory and the role of government in East Asian industrialization*, Princeton, Princeton University Press.

Wade, R., 1990b, 'Industrial policy in East Asia', in G. Gereffi and D. Wyman (eds), *Manufacturing miracles: Patterns of industrialization in Latin America and East Asia*, Princeton, Princeton University Press.

Waterson, Michael, 1984, *Economic theory of the industry*, Cambridge, Cambridge University Press.

Wellicz, S., 1991, 'The Polish case', Symposium on Economic Transition in the Soviet Union and Eastern Europe, *Journal of Economic Perspectives*, 5.

Westphal, L., 1990, 'Industrial policy in an export-propelled economy: lessons from South Korea's experience', *Journal of Economic Perspectives*, 4, 41–59.

White, G., 1988, *Developmental states in East Asia*, London, Macmillan.

Wilhelm, Howard John, 1985, 'The Soviet Union has an administered, not a planned economy', *Soviet Studies*, XXXVII, 118–29.

Williamson, Oliver E., 1964, *The economics of discretionary behaviour: managerial objectives in a theory of the firm*, Englewood Cliffs, Prentice-Hall.

Williamson, Oliver E., 1970, *Corporate control and business behaviour: an inquiry into the effects of organization forms and enterprise behaviour*, Englewood Cliffs, Prentice Hall.

Williamson, Oliver E., 1975, *Markets and hierarchies: analysis and antitrust implications*, New York, Free Press.

Williamson, Oliver E., 1985, *The economic institutions of capitalism: firms, markets, relational contracting*, New York, Free Press.

Wolf, C., 1988, *Markets or governments: choosing between imperfect alternatives*, Cambridge, Mass., MIT Press.

Wolff, E., 1987, *Growth, accumulation and unproductive activity: an analysis of the post-war US economy*, New York, Cambridge University Press.

World Bank, 1991, *World development report 1991, the challenge of development*, Oxford, Oxford University Press.

Zeitlin, M., 1974, 'Corporate ownership and control: the large corporations and the capitalist class', *American Journal of Sociology*, 79, 1073–119.

INDEX

Adam, Gyorgy 83
Adams, W. and Brock, J. 94
Aharoni, Y. 37
Alchian, A.A. and Demsetz, H. 125
Amin, A. and Dietrich, M. 94
Amsden, A. 17, 144
Anchordoghy, M. 162
Aoki, Masahiko 38, 136, 146
Argentina 31, 32, 34
Attaran, M. and Saghafi, M. 94
Australia 31, 32, 33, 62
automobile industry *see* motor
    vehicle industry
Avramovic, D. 170

Baden Württemburg region 142,
    145, 162, 166
Bailey, D., Harte, G. and Sugden, R.
    76, 156, 158
Baran, Paul A. and Sweezy, Paul M.
    42, 47, 48, 110
Barnet, Richard J. and Müller,
    Ronald E. 50
Belgium 11, 33, 61, 68
Benetton company 40
Benson, I. and Lloyd, J. 52
Best, M. 12, 21, 105, 143, 145, 161
Bhaduri, A. and Steindl, J. 109
Bianchi, Patrizio 163, 164
Bils, M. 96
Blackaby, F. 103
Blanchard, O. and Layard, R. 154
Blanchflower, David 83
Blinder, A. 8
BMW corporation 158
Borensztein, E. 20
Brazil 31, 32, 34
British Broadcasting Corporation 134
British Leyland 158, 164
Brusco, S. 145
Buckley, Peter J. and Casson, Mark
    38
Buckley, Peter J. and Enderwick,
    Peter 83

Burkitt, Brian and Bowers, David 78
Bush, George 4

Callaghan, James 95
Camdessus, Michel 20
Canada 31, 32, 33, 62
capitalism vi, 3-4, 169
    full employment and 11
    fundamental problems with 5,
        21-2, 23, 110
    high productivity growth and 11
    inflexibility of 110
    regulation in 8
    in Third World 13
catch-up hypothesis 13, 145
central planning 23, 136-7
centripetalism 22, 52, 56, 58, 59, 67,
    69-70, 72, 74, 127, 128, 129-30,
    132
    and decision structure of capitalist
        firms 23
Charkham, J. 71, 131
Chen, E. 17
China 20, 21, 91, 152
    municipal socialism and small
        scale industry in 18
Chrysler corporation 51, 85, 86
CITER, Emilia Romagna support
    service 161-2
Coase, Ronald H. 37-8, 40, 41, 42,
    125
communications industry 121, 133
community, involvement of in
    decision making 134-8, 147-8,
    163
computer communication networks
    61
consumer electronics 51
Conyon, M. 96
Cosh, A., Hughes, A., Singh, A.,
    Carty, J. and Plender, J. 70
Counter Information Services 78, 86
Cowling, Keith 42, 45, 58, 64, 71, 96,
    101, 141